THE WESTERN FRONT
ILLUSTRATED
1914–1918

THE WESTERN FRONT
ILLUSTRATED
1914–1918

JOHN LAFFIN

Grange
BOOKS

A Sutton Publishing Book

This edition published in 1997 by Grange Books
An imprint of Grange Books plc
The Grange
Grange Yard
London SE1 3AG

British Library Cataloguing in Publication Data
Laffin, John *1992–*
The Western Front illustrated.
1. France. World War I. Military operations
I. Title
940.4144

ISBN 1-84013-007-5

Library of Congress Cataloging in Publication Data
Laffin John.
The Western Front illustrated 1914–1918/John Laffin.
Includes index.
ISBN 0-86299-789-5
1. World War, 1914–1918 Campaigns – Western. I. Title.
D530.L35 1991
940.4'144 – dc20

This book was designed and produced by Alan Sutton Publishing Limited, an imprint of
Sutton Publishing Ltd · Phoenix Mill · Thrupp · Stroud · Gloucestershire

Typeset in 10/14 Times.
Typesetting and origination by
Sutton Publishing Limited.
Printed in Great Britain by
WBC Limited, Bridgend.

CONTENTS

*To the forgotten war illustrators
whose work appears in this book.
Their contribution to the history
of the Great War deserves wider
appreciation*

INTRODUCTION

The Truth of War

A French soldier is hit by a bullet as he struggles through the mud near Bixschoote, in the Ypres Salient. He was taking part in the offensive of 31 July 1917

François Flameng

British soldiers lie dead or dying in the trench after an enemy bombardment. The shell-shard gouges on the tree suggest dreadful wounds to men. The artist has his central figure, the young lieutenant, saying 'Mother! Mother!', and, indeed, many a dying soldier did call to his mother

Alfred Priest

THE TRUTH OF WAR

Relatively few soldiers who survived service on the Western Front were willing to describe their life at the front once the war had finished and they had returned home. For many of them it had been so traumatic and so awful that it was indescribable. So they tried to forget what they had seen; though this was difficult. Also, most quickly sensed that their family and friends did not want to know the grim details of their service, for them a superficial account of the dangers and discomfort was enough.

Even while the war was in progress six volumes of *Deeds that Thrill the Empire* appeared, published by The Standard Art Book Co. of London. They contained 'true stories of the most glorious acts of heroism of the empire's soldiers and sailors during the Great War', all of them written by 'well-known authors'. None of these authors was named but all drew heavily on the published citations which accompanied gallantry awards.

In keeping with the books' title, the illustrations, especially painted for the series, emphasize heroism more than horror, drama more than death, but they were accurate enough in their portrayal of combat. The series did not continue far into 1916, perhaps because by that time battle-

War on the Western Front was mud. Many soldiers who fell into it, sometimes after being wounded, were drowned. Here two soldiers lift a helpless mate from the Somme mud on their rifle slings. Some soldiers had their backs broken during attempts at extrication

Artist unknown

field deeds no longer appeared so boyishly 'thrilling'.

During the 1920s and 1930s, several books of war photographs were published. They showed soldiers' corpses in trenches

A French artist's impression of a victorious Tommy in a captured trench in Picardy, July 1916

J. Simont

There was nothing glamorous about a soldier's uniform on active service. Several illustrators tried to capture the essence of the soldier but few so successfully as in this drawing of the French *poilu* of 1915
Georges Scott

Down the decades, various diaries and memoirs have been published, each one adding something to the great body of knowledge about the Western Front. One of the most honest, informative and moving accounts of war service is, in my opinion, *Unknown Warriors* by Sister K.E. Luard, published in 1930.

All these books were honest attempts to show the reality of the war. The large-format black-cover book *The First World War*, published by the *Daily Express* in 1933, ran an introduction which predicted the reactions of various types of readers:

This is a book which will be looked at not once but a thousand times. Children will gaze at it with curiosity and, as the years go on, with growing understanding. Women still study it with the memory that war is not least cruel to those who stay at home and work, wait and pray. When night comes men will take it from the book-shelf and live

and gunpits, hanging on barbed wire and half-buried in slimy shell-holes. Every page depicted suffering, death or destruction and some children exposed to certain of these books were reported to have suffered nightmares as a result.

A set of three well-produced books was published by The Amalgamated Press, under the editorship of Sir John Hammerton. Under the title *I Was There*, they contain nearly 2,000 pages of first-person accounts of war experiences by soldiers, sailors and airmen. Often with the help of professional editors, the servicemen graphically described their most memorable exploits. Although the truly horrible was omitted from the stories, the dangers and hardships nevertheless still come through clearly.

This fine illustration, from January 1915, shows a veteran advising a very young and apprehensive soldier
Georges Scott

again the days when they played their part in the mad comedy of Armageddon . . . Pacifists will say that the book does not go far enough. Professional soldiers will argue that it stresses the horrors of war and not enough of its splendid adventure . . . He who can look upon this book unmoved is made of firm stuff indeed.

Covenants With Death, published in 1934, and also grimly black-covered, carried the editorial pronouncement: 'The purpose of this book is to reveal the horror, suffering and essential bestiality of modern war, and with that revelation, to warn the nation against the peril of foreign entanglements that must lead Britain to a new Armageddon.'

Made up entirely of photographs, the book carried a full-page warning in large print towards the rear:

The pictures occupying the succeeding fifteen pages are inescapably horrible. But they are essential to a full view of the World War in its phases of terror and bestiality. Highly-strung and sensitive persons may wish to pass them over. And they should not be put in the hands of children. It is important, however, that young folks growing up should understand that they reproduce actual happenings when foreign nations go to war in the floodtide of hate.

Also in the 1930s, interesting 'then and now' books appeared. With the war fifteen years or more in the past, the old battlefields were disappearing, to be replaced by fields and new villages, so that a comparison of past and present was possible. The best of these books was the series *Then And Now*, published by George Newnes in the mid-1930s.

Like Sister Luard, the soldier-poets told the unexpurgated truth of the war at the front. Wilfred Owen, Robert Graves, Edmund Blunden, Siegfried Sassoon, Edward Thomas, Charles Sorley, Laurence

An impression of the horror of the close-quarter fighting in Delville Wood, Longueval, in 1916. The soldiers came to know it grimly as Devil's Wood. Today, the South African memorial graces the peaceful glades

J. Simont

Binyon, Ivor Gurney, David Jones and Isaac Rosenberg all laid bare the stark reality of war. Very few of them glorified war and those who did were writing in 1914 and 1915, before conditions became really frightful. I think it is doubtful that Julian Grenfell, who wrote 'Into Battle' in 1915, would have expressed himself in the same rapturous way had he survived into 1916. Almost certainly the public would not have

received the poem with acclaim in that year of butchery on the battlefield.

The courageous British, Australian, Canadian, French and American official war photographers left many graphic pictures of the war and from every one it is possible to extract information about the many aspects of the soldiers' life and service at the front. Some famous photographs, once generally accepted as having been taken spontaneously, turn out on examination to have been posed, but they are none the less valuable to a military historian.

Under a magnifying glass, hundreds of details become clear in photographs: how soldiers slept, ate and carried out their duties in trenches; what they wore and how they wore it; what stores were kept in dumps, quartermasters' depots and dugouts; the equipment in a casualty clearing station; the dimensions of trenches, and much else.

Progressive images of one French soldier from 1914 to 1917. The fourth illustration seems to imply that this *poilu* has finished his frontline service. The more you look at these paintings, the more detail you pick up

Georges Scott

The work of many of the official war artists adds something to the sum of knowledge but it lacks the detail which would be interesting to the military historian, professional or amateur, and to the countless people who make pilgrimages to the Western Front. Muirhead Bone's work, for instance, is largely sterile. His view of the 'Ruins of the Cloth Hall', in Ypres, fails to give any notion that a war was taking place. His 'Soldiers' Billets – Moonlight'

might be any building at any time in any era. Even 'A Kitchen in the Field' is placid and shows nothing of the rough and ready and urgent activity of an army kitchen preparing food for ravenous soldiers. On the whole, the work left by the official artists is unsatisfactory, though there are significant exceptions.

It is the war illustrators who have left us the most graphic depictions of war on the Western Front. In effect, they were war

British and French soldiers share a cup of wine together – the French water-bottle often contained wine. As they held different sectors, it was relatively rare for the soldiers of the two major Allied armies to come into contact

S. Begg

trenches, small arms and machine-guns and the thousands of objects which collectively make up a battlefield. Some of these men, although completely without army training, had a superb eye for military detail. One illustrator brought to life the scene inside a German blockhouse at the moment of its surrender to Australian soldiers. No photographer was ever able to be on the spot for such an occasion. Another imagined himself behind a German machine-gunner and painted the scene as a British soldier rushed him with rifle and bayonet. A third depicted the havoc caused by a shell exploding in a trench in a way that was, naturally, impossible for a photographer.

The illustrators had other advantages over photographers. To achieve greater clarity or dramatic emphasis, they could juxtapose an individual soldier or group of men with a particular background; in their artistic imagination, they could hover above a trench during a raid; they might place themselves flank-on while an attack was being made; and they could reveal what was taking place in the gloom of No Man's Land at night. In brief, they drew or painted from the most advantageous position possible, while the photographer worked from wherever he could. There was a big difference.

As a boy, I grew up among war veterans, including both my parents. My mother was an army nursing sister, my father an infantry officer. By great good fortune I was trained, in the early years of World War II, by instructors who had been infantry officers, NCOs and private soldiers during the previous Great War. I and my comrades dug trenches to their specifications, erected barbed-wire obstacles – and learned how to destroy enemy wire – practised raids by day

correspondents with pen, pencil, charcoal and brush. Not all of them actually visited the battlefields, but they could do what few photographers ever had the opportunity to do – illustrate scenes of battle because they frequently had contact with soldiers on the ground. Photographers and cameramen on occasions, such as on the first day of the Somme, 1 July 1916, recorded pre-battle scenes, but taking pictures or film in the fury of battle was virtually impossible.

It was equally rare for the artists to be present during combat, although several of them did accurately depict battle and the battle front. The best of them interviewed eyewitnesses and survivors and while doing so made rough drawings.

While visiting the front and the areas close to it, the illustrators made reference sketches of guns, limbers, wagons, dugouts,

Another splendid drawing of a youthful French soldier with a group of older men, in a battered village just behind the lines in August 1916. The small rolls of material on the men's shoulders are to prevent equipment or rifle sling from slipping off

J. Simont

and by night, and became imbued with the art and science and improvisation of war. These veterans were teaching us *their* war. Even our training manuals were full of lessons from their war. This is one reason why I am able to recognize the work of the war illustrators as accurate.

This book almost entirely depicts the work of war illustrators. In many cases I have taken a detail from a larger piece of work in order to draw attention to the topic I am discussing. The war illustrators' work is graphic and with minor exceptions it was accurate, yet it seems never to have been regarded as a serious testimony of war. One retired senior official of the Imperial War Museum to whom I put this point said, 'They were merely illustrators, not real artists, so they can't be taken seriously.' This appears to be an illogical statement and I believe the work of the war illustrators should be given serious consideration.

I feel, as a military historian, rather than as an art critic, the best of the illustrators were Fortunino Matania, Harry Payne, Caton Woodville, Lucien Jonas, Georges Scott and J. Simont. Among the most prolific were Margaret Dovaston, W. Avis, S.T. Dadd, J.H. Valda, H. Ripperger, E.A. Holloway and W.S. Bagdatopulas, all of whom were illustrators for *Deeds that Thrill the Empire*. All produced dramatic drawings, but they lacked the finesse of the great war illustrators.

Many of the artists died in the 1920s and most were dead by 1940. A number of them disappeared – professionally at least – after 1918, almost as if the end of the war had deprived them of a reason to go on working. The most durable of the great illustrators was Fortunino Matania, who worked during the war for *The Illustrated London News*,

Life was not always unpleasant in the war zone. Away from the trenches and in billets soldiers relaxed and even enjoyed themselves in the company of their French or Flemish hosts. A scene in a farmhouse in northern France in 1917.

S. Ugo

Not No Man's Land exactly, but a shell-wrecked French village evacuated by its inhabitants. Two British cavalrymen on patrol find a lost infant in the wreckage. A veteran illustrator was on hand, in 1917, to record the scene

Harry Payne

The Sphere, the French *L'Illustration*, the British government and for various regiments. He then flourished in other artistic fields until his death in 1963. I am grateful to his nephew Franco Matania, himself an artist, for permission to reproduce his work. I regard Matania as incomparably the best of the war illustrators in clarity, military accuracy and attention to detail.

Matania was born in Naples, and by the age of twenty he was working in Paris; soon after he moved to London. Following three years with *The Graphic* he returned to Italy to complete his national military service, a period which gave him an insight into mili-

tary life. Returning to London, he worked for *The Sphere* and, so accurate was he in portraying royal occasions, that he was invited to cover the Delhi Durbar of 1911 when King George V and Queen Mary were installed as King-Emperor and Queen-Empress of India. Matania received the Durbar Medal for his services.

The outbreak of the Great War gave Matania many opportunities for his talents. Employed by the Ministry of Propaganda, he visited the front several times. His skill and his photographic memory combined to produce work remarkable in its richness of detail. When he judged that his own experience was insufficient to deal with a subject he talked about it to soldiers. Sometimes he would visit a wounded man in hospital, taking with him sketches and a box of toy soldiers to use as artistic props. Working deftly and swiftly, Matania could finish a complex painting in a few days. When he was not producing work for magazines, he fulfilled commissions from regiments. For the Royal Munster Fusiliers he painted 'The Absolution on the Rue du Bois', when the chaplain blessed the troops before an action of May 1915.

The war illustrators whose work appears in this book are:

British

W. Avis (no trace), J.P. Beadle (1863–1947), S. Begg (no trace), Montague Black (no trace), J.P. Campbell (no trace), Christopher Clark (1875–1942), G. Crosby (1885–1940), S.T. Dadd (no trace), Margaret Dovaston (1872–1940), Francis E. Hiley (no trace), E.A. Holloway (no trace), Fortunino Matania (1881–1963), D. McPherson (1871–

1930), Harry Payne (1868–1940), A. Pearse (no trace), Alfred Priest (1874–1929), H. Ripperger (no trace), J.H. Valda (no trace), W.B. Wollen (1857–1936), R. Caton Woodville (1856–1927).

French

John de G. Bryan (no trace), S. Eduardo (no trace), Frederic de Harnen (1866–1928), François Flameng (no trace), A. Forestier (1854–1930), Lucien Jonas (1880–1940), A. de Parys (no trace), Georges Scott (1878–1948), J. Simont (no trace), Joseph Simpson (1879–1939), S. Ugo (no trace).

American

Wallace Coop (no trace), Charles W. Wyllie (1853–1923).

German

H. Moloff (no trace).

As with all my books, I owe my wife, Hazelle, a considerable debt of gratitude for practical help with this one. She has thirty-five years of Western Front 'service'. I am also grateful to Doreen Hall of the Powys County Library, and to David Cohen, for their help in tracing details of the war illustrators.

CHAPTER 1

*The Trenches; Trenches and
Breastworks as Constructions;
The Trench System and Manning; Trench Life*

In an offensive late in 1916, men of the Naval Division charge
down from the Schwaben Height to attack the Germans in
position near St Pierre Divion. This was part of the Somme
battlefield near Albert

John de G. Brian

A young French soldier, Mathieu Jouy, holds a trench single-handed after all his comrades have fallen. Several times wounded, he held out until help arrived and survived the action, which took place early in 1915

J. Simont

THE TRENCHES

The history of the Great War on the Western Front is almost entirely one of trench warfare. Every aspect of this great conflict is linked to the trenches – strategy and tactics, the suffering and casualties, confusion and chaos, courage and endurance, mythology and legend. From 1915, the very term *the trenches* was synonymous with the war itself and service in them profoundly affected every frontline soldier of every nation. The many soldiers who wrote of their experiences give more space to their time in the trenches than to any other part of their service, yet most men spent longer out of the trenches than in them. The explanation is that the trenches produced an intensity of horror and of emotion that overwhelmed all the other experiences of a soldier's life, especially the life of the infantryman.

I.S. Bloch, a Polish banker and economist, writing in 1897, warned that the development of industrialization would fundamentally alter the character of war. Bloch stated that the outward and visible sign of the end of the old style of warfare was the introduction of the magazine rifle. The soldier, by perfecting the mechanism of slaughter, had practically brought about his own extinction. I.S. Bloch's vivid description of how a new war in Europe would be fought was to prove uncannily accurate:

At first there will be increased slaughter on so terrible scale as to render it impossible to get troops to push the battle to a decisive issue. They will try to, thinking that they are fighting under the old conditions, and they will learn such a lesson that they will abandon the attempt. The war, instead of being a hand-to-hand contest in which the combatants measure their physical and moral superiority, will become a kind of stalemate, in which neither army being able to get at the other, both armies will be maintained in opposition to each other, threatening each other, but never being able to deliver a final and decisive blow. Everybody will be entrenched in the next war; the spade will be as indispensable to the soldier as his rifle.

Bloch, a civilian, had studied the previous half a century of armed conflict in the American Civil War, the Franco-Prussian War and the Russo-Japanese war, among others. He could see the inevitable looming but the European generals were blind to it.

For the many people who are today interested in the Great War, if any one word or one concept evokes more images of the war than others it must be 'trenches'. Descriptions of men existing in trenches, fighting and dying in them, permeates the literature of the war. The very phrase 'trench warfare' conjures up images of carnage and horror and the photographic files of the great libraries contain more pictures of trenches than of any other aspect of the war. In turn, these still photographs have formed the basis of television documentaries about the war. Understandably, photographs of actual combat in trenches are almost non-existent, so that we have to rely on the informed imagination of the war illustrators. Some of their creations are not only graphic but accurate reconstructions of trench fighting.

An understanding of the Great War begins with an understanding of trenches – why they came into existence, the different types of trenches and how they were made and used. To describe 'the trenches' I have divided the subject into three sections: trenches and breastworks as constructions; the trench system and manning; and trench life.

TRENCHES AND BREASTWORKS AS CONSTRUCTIONS

The war began in August 1914, and was initially a war of movement, with the great French and German armies manoeuvring over large areas of Belgium and France as they strove to gain an advantage. The British Expeditionary Force joined the French and it too was at first involved in a march–fight–retreat type of war. The German armies, although powerful, could not break through to Paris and the French Channel ports. The equally large, but more old-fashioned French armies could not drive back the invaders, only block them. By the end of October all the military leaders realized that war by manoeuvre, with large forces of cavalry screening the movement of infantry corps, had come to an end. Each side needed continuous lines of defence in order to prevent the other side from out-flanking them.

That winter, both sides worked almost incessantly to create an unbroken front from the Swiss border to the Belgian coast on the English Channel, a distance of 400 miles. They achieved this by linking countless established positions, large and small, with trenches and breastworks. The largest position was the French fortress of Verdun, while small posts proliferated, some of them nothing more than shell-holes which had been roughly fortified to make a strong-point. In some places the opposing front lines were a mile apart, in others only a few hundred yards and elsewhere on either side of a river. At many parts of the front only about thirty yards separated the French and British armies from the Germans.

Most soldiers, from senior officers down to ordinary men in the ranks, expected that war and life in the trenches would last only for the winter. 'This will tide us over until the spring', many men said. They were all aware of the European military tradition that armies 'settled down' in winter because of the difficulties of movement and supply. Fighting always resumed in the spring, with

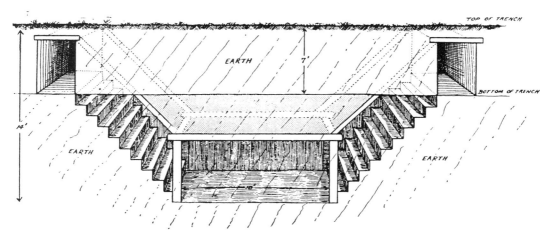

A type of German dugout under the frontline trench, as illustrated in a British manual

the troops leaving their winter quarters and resuming open warfare. Throughout the winter of 1914–15, many soldiers lived with this anticipation.

In the meantime, the French and Germans massed howitzers, heavy guns and trench mortars to defend their positions. Both armies were accustomed to fortress and siege operations. The British Expeditionary Force had few such weapons; the troops were unskilled in preparing trenches and, on manoeuvres before the war, the infantry were required to return and fill in any trenches they might have dug. As a result, soldiers tried to avoid having to dig them.

As the trench system developed during that first winter the trenches were widened to about 7 ft at the top and perhaps 3 ft at the bottom, though some at 2 ft were uncomfortably narrow. The depth was between 6 ft 6 in and 7 ft. So that the troops could fire over or through the parapet, a fire-step was dug into the forward side of the trench. The fire-step was 2 or 3 ft high. It was on this that the sentries stood – or the whole unit when standing-to – in order to confront an anticipated enemy attack.

The parados was supposed to be built higher than the parapet so that the defenders were not outlined against the sky and were therefore not such easy targets. The parados had a second benefit; it protected the frontline troops against those firing from the support trench or elsewhere in the rear. Some soldiers said sourly that the parados rather than the parapet was more frequently the reason for their survival.

Draining the trenches was a major problem that was never satisfactorily solved. Pumps of various sizes were introduced but none was ever powerful enough to take out the water. In any case, even when the water was siphoned out of one trench system it ran into another. Many a British soldier received from home personal trench pumps which his loved ones hoped would keep his feet dry – they didn't.

The armies soon found that the sides of trenches needed strengthening, especially in soft soil and in wet weather. Revetments of timber, wattling and sandbags were successfully used, provided that the revetments were continually repaired. Millions of sandbags arrived at the front and became the

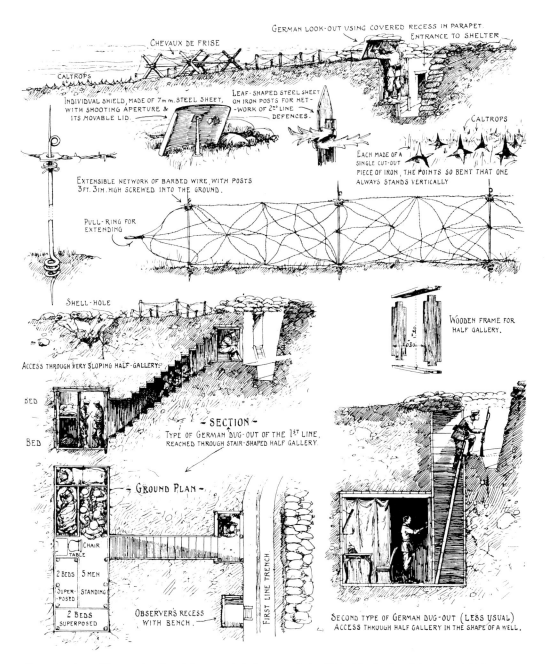

These drawings of German frontline defences and shelters were first published by the French in August 1915. They prove that even at this early period the Germans were securely settled

Artist unknown

most commonly used form of strengthening trenches. Many German trenches were lined on the front or battle side with sheet steel instead of sandbags.

The British army formed entrenching battalions to help pioneers, engineers and infantry construct trench systems. Trench digging was desperately hard work but it had the benefit of being good exercise and most soldiers, though they hated digging, owed their basic fitness to it.

The terrain of Flanders posed special problems for defence. The land was generally so low that the water-table lay only 18 in and at most 3 ft below the surface. Even in peacetime large areas could only be used for farming because they were drained by a complex system of ditches.

The army did not understand the problem in 1914 and when digging was first tried the troops who garrisoned the resulting 'trenches' found themselves standing in gluey mud which reached above the boot and often up to the knee. This quickly led to trench foot and other ailments. Drains and pumps were tried; the drains worsened the problem and the pumps were useless.

The only solution was to build breastworks on top of the water-logged ground instead of digging holes into it. These breastworks were often referred to as command or parapet trenches while the Germans called them box trenches. They required enormous effort and vast amounts of material to construct.

In effect, breastworks were above-ground trenches. Earth, mud, rocks, tree trunks and branches and wreckage of all kinds was piled up to provide cover more than 8 ft high. The breastworks facing the enemy were sometimes 20–30 ft through, with deep rear walls as well. Due to their substantial

nature, dugouts could be burrowed into them, just as they were into ordinary trenches.

Communication trenches in the flat, water-logged lands were built in the same way, above ground. In the many places where communication trenches crossed ditches and narrow streams they were built up on platforms. Without this protection, soldiers using the communication trenches would have been vulnerable to enemy machine-gunners who would have been able to set up their weapons to cover such open spaces.

The British at first gave practically no thought to overhead trench cover, though this would have made life much more bearable for the troops. Even half cover, extending at right angles from the parados, would have given some protection from rain, wind and snow. Soldiers soon learned to scrape out a 'funk' hole from the side of the trench, but such holes were more effective in summer and in chalk rather than in softer earth. It was possible to curl up in a 'funk' hole to snatch some sleep and many soldiers managed to drape a waterproof sheet over the opening as some protection from rain.

From 1916, many support and reserve trenches were covered for long stretches with corrugated iron or wood. In the British frontline trenches there was never satisfactory headcover, but much depended on the initiative of individual battalion officers. Some, at their own expense, supplied awnings which could be quickly fixed above support and reserve trenches in wet weather. Their men blessed them for such consideration.

The quantities of material used in making and strengthening those trench systems were prodigious. On a single reserve trench

The French artist entitled this drawing 'Le froid dans la Somme'. Millions of men could testify to the freezing conditions

Lucien Jonas

line on a brigade front of 2,000 yd near La Bassée, the 42nd East Lancashire Division used 5,036 bags of cement, 19,384 bags of shingle and 9,692 bags of sand, a total weight of 1,000 tons.

Sandbags

Preparing sandbags was as meticulously carried out as any other army activity. A filling party was supposed to consist of three men, one shovelling the earth in and two holding and tying the bags. The men stacking the filled bags worked in pairs at a required rate of sixty bags an hour, but all concerned were capable of much greater speed in an emergency. A skilled filling team put the same amount of earth into each bag, so that it was three-quarters filled.

After tying, it was shovel-beaten into a rectangle 30 in × 10 in × 5 in.

The construction of sandbag defences was by 'English bond'. This meant a course of 'headers', laid at right angles to the face, and then a course of 'stretchers', with the longer side parallel to the wall. The 'chokes' or tied ends of the bags were closed away from the trench, leaving a seamless face on the inside wall of the trench. Sometimes, when the supply of sandbags was inadequate, the men's packs were filled with earth and stacked sandbag fashion.

Thick defences were needed if only because of the penetrative power of the 1914–18 pointed bullet. Army instruction manuals gave these measurements of penetration: brickwork, 9–14 in; chalk, 15 in;

One of the most appealing drawings to come out of the trenches. Umbrellas were certainly not army issue but understanding officers tolerated them, at least in March 1916

S. Begg

sand in bags, 18 in; loose earth, 30 in; hardwood, 38 in; stone-free earth, 40 in; soft wood, 58 in; clay, 60 in; dry turf or peat, 80 in.

Many photographs taken during the war show trenches in a state of destruction after heavy bombardment. Also, after heavy rain and much infantry movement they would be reduced to an appalling state. However, trenches were by no means haphazard in construction nor was their upkeep neglected by the troops manning them. The quality of trench maintenance varied according to the training and discipline of the units in them, but on the whole junior officers and senior NCOs saw to it that they remained in good shape. The unit's battle efficiency depended on it. In 'normal' times – when the enemy was not engaged in heavy bombardment in readiness for an attack and when the weather was reasonable – the trenches were orderly, with many signposts to indicate the position of various HQs, the regimental aid posts, bomb stores, latrine and so on.

The memoirs of some British soldiers give the impression, now strongly held by people interested in the Western Front, that whenever British units took over French trenches they found them filthy and insanitary. Certainly, the French lived too close to their latrines – sometimes their dugouts were over them. However, French

ELEVATION. SECTION.

I. SANDBAG REVETMENT SHEWING COMMON FAULTS. VIZ :–
PLUMB FACE. ALL BAGS LAID AS STRETCHERS. JOINTS NOT PROPERLY BROKEN. HORIZONTAL COURSING NOT MAINTAINED. BAGS UNEVENLY FILLED. DANGEROUS STRETCHER BAG ON TOP. INADEQUATE SOIL BACKING TO PARAPET. BOTTOM COURSE ABOVE TRENCH FLOOR. BAGS NOT SPADED SQUARE.

ELEVATION SECTION.

II. SANBAG REVETMENT SHEWING RIGHT METHOD. NOTE :–
"4 IN.1" BATTER BACK OF FACE. HEADER COURSE TOP AND BOTTOM. SUNK FOUNDATION WITH BOTTOM PERPENDICULAR TO FACE. EVENLY FILLED BAGS WELL SQUARED AND LAID BY SPADE SLAPS BONDING WITH HEADER BAGS ALTERNATELY WITH STRETCHERS HAVING JOINTS REGULARLY BROKEN AS IN BRICKWORK. THE TOP SHOULD BE GIVEN AN IRREGULAR LINE BY THROWING A FEW OLD SANDBAGS ON TOP AT INTERVALS. THESE ARE MERELY TO BREAK UP THE OUTLINE AND ARE NOT TO BE REGUARDED AS IN ANY WAY STRENGTHENING THE PARAPET.

A page from an army instructional manual of January 1916, complete with mis-spellings

dugouts were generally roomier than the British and French construction was usually superior to the British, though still inferior to the Germans. The French used a permanent staff to build and maintain communication trenches, hence these workers had a thorough knowledge of their front and an interest in good work. The British system was to use Royal Engineer officers and NCOs and infantry working parties, all of which came and went with their brigades.

THE TRENCH SYSTEM AND MANNING

Some historians consider that 'trench warfare proper' began in September 1914 when the German Reserve Corps blocked the advance of the British 1st Corps on Chemin des Dames ridge, in the Champagne sector. This might have been the beginning of the stalemate but no trench warfare 'proper' was possible before a trench system had been dug. This took place during the late autumn of 1914 and the entire winter of 1914–15.

By mid-1916, for every mile of front, the British and French had a total length of 30 miles of trenches, running parallel to the front or at right-angles to it. It is impossible to calculate the number of man-hours spent in creating the entire trench system, but some idea of the labour required may be gauged by a single statistic – the 10 million spades and shovels issued to the British army in just one year, 1918.

Private Victor Wheeler, a Canadian, describes the dismay of French peasants as they saw the soldiers despoil their farms by digging trenches:

With pick and shovel we dug trenches through beautiful fields of grain, fully realising what damage we were doing to *les fermiers*' hope of reaping small harvests that would enable them to stem hunger during the coming winter. The patriarch with his ox-drawn plough, the matronly gleaner, and the young woman gathering grass and leaves, roots and truffles, stood arms akimbo, wordlessly, helplessly, hopelessly watching. The depressing effect on the morale of the men – to many of whom raising grain on the Western prairie also meant their livelihood – could not be easily dismissed.

The British trench system usually consisted of a spread of barbed wire, then three lines of trenches – front, support and reserve – covering a depth of between 200 and 500 yd. The three lines were linked to one another by communication trenches so that, in theory, it was not necessary for men to have to expose themselves above ground.

Trenches could not be dug in long straight lines. The danger was obvious. Should the enemy break into the defences they could simply shoot straight along the trenches, that is, they could enfilade the defenders. To obviate this, each trench was dug with alternate fire-bays and traverses. The straight sections were the fire-bays, from where the troops did their shooting. Each fire-bay was screened from the next by a barrier of earth and sandbags and joining the two was a traverse. The British and Germans had the same system of right-angled traverses and fire-bays for their fighting trenches, but the French preferred straightforward continuous zig-zags. They were easier to dig but they also provided less protection. British and Empire troops were never happy when taking over French positions because they did not feel safe enough.

The ideal trench system rarely existed on any part of the long front. On some stretches, the intensity of fighting prevented

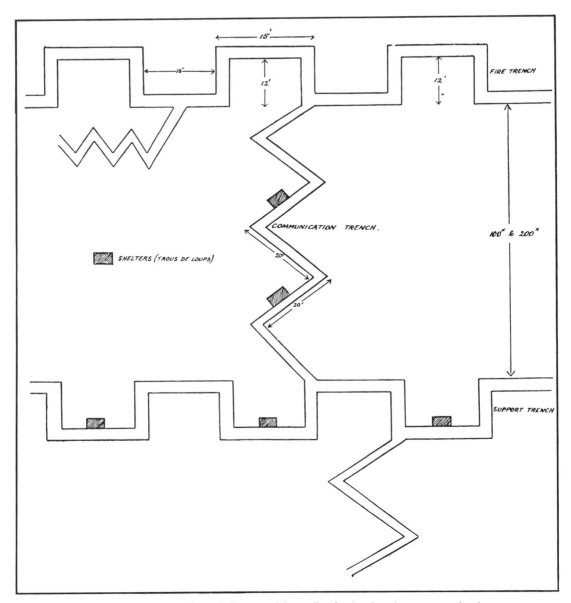

A diagram of an ideal trench layout, as shown in the manual. In practice, few trench systems were as sharply angular as this one

a properly integrated system from being established. Difficult country, rocky terrain and adverse digging conditions resulted in many trenches being straighter for longer lengths than laid down in orders.

History books speak superficially of 'a continuous line of trenches' but in winter, and especially during combat in this season, the frontline deteriorated into nothing more than an uneven line of mudholes. Because of lack of time and opportunity, constant harassing shell-fire, rain and the men's exhaustion, existing trenches could not be revetted and they collapsed.

The British High Command had ordered that no frontline battalion should ever give ground voluntarily. This handicapped local commanders, who often saw ways in which they could improve their tactical position but were prevented from doing so by this order. On many occasions, by retiring from a small piece of useless terrain an officer could have been in a better position in relation to an adjoining battalion. Similarly, he might have been able to take up new positions on higher ground. However, the order remained that no rearward movement could be made for purely tactical reasons. This policy meant that many German salients, small and large, protruded into the British lines. Vimy Ridge was a classic example, until its capture in April 1917. The British High Command ordered many costly, and generally useless, assaults to pluck out the enemy salients. In the meantime, they provided excellent command and observation positions for the Germans.

The Germans called their elaborate defensive positions *stellungs*. Just seven of them made up the front, the most famous being the Siegfried *stellung*, from Cambrai to St Quentin. The trench system, even without the remarkable underground defences, was formidable. It had a greater depth than the British and French systems, with up to ten lines of traversed trenches. In addition, the Germans had switch trenches. These usually ran diagonally from the frontline trench to the support trench. Should the defenders be forced out of the frontline they ran to the switch line. From this oblique position, they could mow down the enemy infantry who had captured their front trench and were moving onto the support trench. It

was a simple and effective extra form of defence. German wire was generally fixed in broader bands than that of the British and French.

Protected by machine-guns (see separate section) a trench system was virtually impregnable to infantry attack. By great gallantry and after suffering heavy losses some soldiers would capture a frontline trench, even a support trench, but it was almost impossible for infantry to breach a trench system by frontal assault.

General Hindenburg, once he became German supreme commander in 1917, insisted on defence in great depth, with a network of lines and groups of strong points. 'In the deep cones thus formed', he later wrote, 'we did not intend to dispose our troops on a rigid and continuous front but in a complex system of nuclei [by which he meant strongpoints] and distributed in breadth and depth.' He conceived the sensible idea of voluntarily abandoning parts of the line which he could no longer hold and then mounting counter-attacks to recover points which were essential to maintaining the whole position.

Communication Trenches

Communication trenches were the nerve system of the defence complex. While the fighting trenches ran parallel to the front, the communication trenches were dug at right-angles to it. From the rear, perhaps 2 or 3 miles distant, they crossed the reserve and support lines and finally reached the frontline. The French name for communication trench was *boyau*, meaning 'gut' some British units habitually referred to these trenches as 'boy-ohs'. In a real sense, communication trenches were the guts of the battlefield, especially in British sectors.

The French used tramways right up to the support line in many places and always to the reserve line. This practice meant that supplies could be delivered in quantity. The British manhandled everything along the communication trenches – or when possible in the open – with consequent exhaustion, as well as inadequacy and unreliability of supply.

Communication trenches were always busy, especially at night. Carrying parties took supplies of water, food, ammunition, bombs and trench stores up to the front. Wounded men, walking or on stretchers, were sent out, as well as others called back to HQ for one reason or another. Sometimes a man's leave became due while he was in the frontline and he would be ordered away. Trench reliefs were carried out along the communicating trenches. On a dark night, heavily encumbered men collided with one another and their equipment became entangled, leading to exasperated swearing. Many a soldier slipped on mud, fell and brought down some of his mates in angry heaps.

A man of the 10th Battalion York and Lancaster Regiment stumbled into a shell-hole and was held fast by the mud and slime. He was buried up to his chest and attempts to haul him out by ropes would have killed him. Pioneers worked for four nights to free him, while his mate remained with him day and night under fire, occasionally putting food in his mouth from a long stick. Both men were delirious by the time the victim was eventually freed. Such was the power of the mud.

Occasionally, a communication trench was partly traversed, fire-stepped, loop-holed and wired to form a defensive flank in an emergency. Actually, such a trench generally indicated that some Allied unit so distrusted the neighbouring foreign unit that it felt that flank protection was needed.

For all soldiers, the trench system was so complex that even veterans managed to lose themselves occasionally. Entire units, on their way by night to relieve a particular part of the frontline, blundered about for hours in their efforts to find it. Guides familiar with certain sectors were supposed to lead in the relieving troops but even they lost their way. When captured enemy trenches were incorporated into a system, soldiers of both sides could find themselves in hostile territory. On one occasion a German mail clerk with a full sack of letters walked right through the Canadian frontline network and reached the support line before being stopped and taken prisoner.

Manning the Line

Much debate took place about the manning of trenches. In 1915 and for much of 1916 the British heavily manned their frontline, hoping to stop a German attack at the wire or in No Man's Land. Inevitably, many defenders were killed during heavy bombardments and, when the enemy broke through, others were captured. Innumerable variations in manning were tried. The French had an imaginative idea as early as 1915. They created alternate 'active' and 'passive' sections in their frontline. The active zone was strongly manned while the passive zone was held by only a few men, but more heavily wired. Also, support companies were more strongly in place behind the passive fronts than the active zones. When the Germans attacked they naturally made more progress against the French passive zones, but as they struggled to get through the wire they came under deadly flanking fire. On occasions, the resolute German infantry broke through, only to run against the French *arrêt-ligne* or stop-line. Here, every French defender was under orders to fight to the death.

The British army did not carry out any similar systematic experiments and simply covered each part of the front with a trench system that seemed best suited at the time. The British over manned the frontline for most of the war. Soldiers stood practically shoulder to shoulder and consequently died in large numbers during an enemy bombardment. This policy applied even as late as spring 1918 when the great German offensive opened. During the tremendous artillery onslaught, British casualties were heavy. The mobile reserve, under this rigid system, was about one-third of the fighting strength.

The French and German trench-manning systems had developed – while the British remained static – with a forward zone, battle zone and rear zone. None of them had rigid trench lines but groups of mutually supporting posts, whether of infantry or machine-guns. Sometimes these posts were a quarter of a mile apart. Not surprisingly, casualties from artillery fire were far fewer. Most importantly, the Germans held two-thirds of their fighting strength for counter-attack or exploitation. The French copied the system and later so did the British, but their reserve was never more than one-third.

L. Pips
Most people think of the frontline trench as the most exposed position on the battlefield but this is an erroneous belief. Running out at right-angles from the front trench were

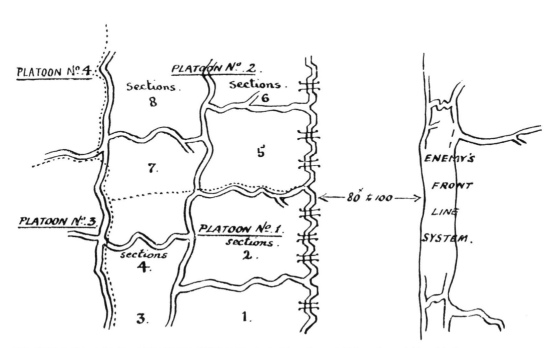

This diagram shows the four platoons of a 1916 company and how they might have been deployed in the trenches

saps – narrow, shallow slit trenches – towards L. Pips (listening posts), where life was always hazardous. Perhaps 30 yd in front of the trench, these posts were extremely dangerous for the two or three men in them. From their small posts, most of which had been adapted from shell-holes, they peered into the dark, while straining to hear any sounds from the enemy lines, noises which might indicate an approaching patrol, a wiring party at work, or a sniper slithering into position before dawn.

During a bombardment, some shells would fall in No Man's Land and even before the bombardment had died down both sides would send out men to seize any new craters which could be used as listening posts. From August 1916 until April 1917 all British units were under orders to occupy any shell-hole within 60 yd of their forward trench. Some local commanders drove two saps to a hole, at right-angles. Such positions became known as cruciform posts because they were at the junction of two arms of a cross.

Latrines

Practically nothing has been written about latrines, but they were an important part of a trench system. Latrines were dug at the end of short saps, mostly to the rear of trenches but, in the case of the frontline, sometimes forward. This idea seems to have been based on the belief that a soldier forward of his main line would be less likely to linger than one who had gone to the rear. Before a change-over in the trenches, an outgoing unit was supposed to fill in its latrines and dig a new one for the fresh arrivals.

Some officers, worried about the dangers of disease, had strict rules about use of latrines; defecating in a fighting trench or communication trench could result in punishment.

By regulation, trench latrines were supposed to be pits dug 4 ft to 5 ft deep, in a special sap. When filled to within a foot of the top they were filled in and a new one dug. The actual practice varied greatly. At various times metal buckets were used, again in a special sap. Instructions were that when filled the contents of the buckets were to be buried between the front and support trenches but often as not soldiers simply threw it as far as possible. Shell-holes were frequently used as latrines. Each company had two 'sanitary personnel' – generally called 'shit wallahs' – whose job it was to dispose of urine and excreta. This is something not mentioned in most history books. Nor is the fact that many a latrine was a 'two-holer', which soldiers considered superior to a 'one-holer' because mates could sit side by side and chat.

Sanitary duty was reserved in many units as a punishment for defaulters. The repulsive job was objectionable and humiliating and it caused individual defiance. In a few cases it led to desertion.

Some soldiers, and probably even more officers, habitually went out into No Man's Land at night where they used a shell-hole or a hollow as a latrine. This practice was considered dangerous and was against regulations, but those who did it were men who preferred the privacy and the relative lack of smell in No Man's Land. Generally, they took the precaution of telling the sentry that they were 'just popping over the top for a minute'. Even so, some were shot as they crept back, mistaken by a tense sentry for an enemy scout or raider.

A young French veteran, already twice decorated, gives a lesson in observation to a soldier new to the trenches.
The uniforms show the period to be very early in 1915

Georges Scott

TRENCH LIFE

The frontline soldiers of the Great War, after one spell in the trenches, dreaded having to return to them. During their tour of duty there, they lived in great discomfort and considerable tension, and hours before they were due to be relieved by another unit they worried about something happening to delay the change-over. In short, the trenches dominated the soldier's life, even when he wasn't actually in them. Any impression that soldiers were safe in the trenches, even if they were miserably uncomfortable, is wrong. Possibly one-third of all casualties on the Western Front, in the Allied armies, were killed or wounded in the trenches, mostly from artillery fire.

On paper, an infantry battalion's routine seemed simple enough and well organized. It amounted to a spell in the frontline, a period in support and then in reserve and, after a short rest, back to the front. In practice, there were wildly differing interpretations of this 'system'. Also, being 'in support' or 'at rest' had no precise meanings. Much depended on GHQ, Army or Corps HQ or Divisional HQ and on particular commanders and their staffs. For them, the exigencies of the moment took precedence over any supposed system.

Any modern person interested in life on the Western Front needs to be aware that no one pattern existed and that soldiers writing about being 'in the line', or anywhere else, had individual perceptions of the phrases they used. Even 'in the line' in soldiers' descriptions does not necessarily mean in the fire trench; it could mean in the support trench or the reserve trench.

Actual examples give some idea of the various lengths of time spent on particular duties. In 1916, Lieutenant Charles Carrington, of the Warwickshire Regiment, analysed his diary for the year. He had spent sixty five days in the frontline and thirty six more in supporting positions 'close at hand'. He had 120 days in reserve positions close enough to the line to reach it on foot when the occasion demanded. A total of seventy three days were spent 'at rest', seventeen days on leave and ten days in hospital. During his 101 days under fire he had twelve tours of duty in the trenches, varying in length from one to thirteen days.

The 13th Yorks and Lancs spent fifty one consecutive days in the line and the West Yorks endured seventy out of ninety days in the trenches, though not consecutively. Finding the 'record' for the time spent without relief in the trenches would be a difficult and perhaps impossible task.

Stand-to!
The routine of trench life was based on the stand-to and the stand-down. One hour before dawn every morning, the orderly officer and orderly sergeant of each company gave the order to 'Stand-to!' Still half-asleep, the shivering, aching men clambered onto the fire-step, clutching their rifles with bayonets fixed. This was the time when an enemy attack was considered most likely so both sides fully manned the trenches. Sometimes a 'morning hate' accompanied the

This is the only photograph in the book. Taken in a communications trench by a French photographer in the Argonne, it shows the difficulty of evacuating wounded men. One soldier had set off to walk to the aid post but collapsed and may be dead

A soldier uses a small rifle periscope to spot enemy movement

Artist unknown

stand-to, with a furious firing of rifles and machine-guns. This was supposed to block any enemy attempt to approach through the gloom and mist but after a while the hate became almost a custom, to be carried out for its own sake. After an hour had passed and the light was good, the order was given to 'Stand-down!' and only the sentries remained on the alert. Then breakfast began the real trench day.

An hour before dark a second stand-to was ordered, since this period was also considered dangerous, especially while dusk was settling over the fields. Both sides knew the other's trench routine so it might seem surprising that attacks were mounted when the defences were known to be on a state of highest alert. Nevertheless, many attacks *were* made during these periods, especially when field intelligence reports indicated that trenches were held by raw units.

On most sectors at some time or another the opposing troops reached a friendly, if unofficial, understanding. Then neither side commenced shelling before 8 a.m., so that all soldiers could have a comfortable breakfast and were better able to face the dangers of the day. Usually, this arrangement extended to never shelling the transport, since this made life in the trenches all the more uncomfortable by destroying stores and food. Such periods were short-lived and they always came to an end when a senior officer got wind of a sector of his front being unduly peaceful.

The degree of discomfort depended on the season, the weather and the extent to which trenches were smashed by enemy guns. Some periods and some sectors were appalling. For instance, in the winter of 1916–17, on the Somme front, there were no 'proper' trenches, only weather-eroded muddy ditches.

Officers and men realized that there was no point in improving the trenches because the mud would collapse them or within hours enemy guns would smash them. Some trenches had no barbed-wire cover because the soldiers of both sides were incapable of moving, let alone erecting wire. Wet through from constant drizzle, freezing cold and desperate for a hot meal, the miserable men huddled under whatever shelter they could scratch together. Soldiering was just a matter of enduring until the relief unit arrived. Should an attack have been contemplated, the slime prevented the men from climbing out of the trenches. So did the absence of wooden ladders, which the frozen men burned in an attempt to keep warm. Duckboards, burial crosses and even the hard-issue biscuits were used for the same purpose.

Those men who could endure no more stood up, invited the sniper's bullet and invariably received it. Snipers were the only soldiers still in action on both sides. A change-over at the end of a period in the line was always dangerous and those on their way in or out came under artillery fire as well as fire from machine-guns firing on fixed lines along a track or across gaps.

High explosive shells bursting in the confines of a trench had devastating effects, mutilating men, destroying equipment and blocking the trench with rubble. While this was the general effect, in reality, no two shells caused precisely the same damage. An explosion could kill four men in a group and leave the fifth shaken but unscathed. A shell that dropped to the floor of the trench and penetrated a little way might do nothing more than create a hole, but one that exploded on impact would send shell-shards at great velocity in both directions along the trench. Soldiers were forever talking about lucky escapes.

Edmund Blunden was one of the most painfully honest of observers, as he shows in this description of the horror caused by a shell-burst in a trench: 'Its impression was black and stinking where three minutes ago the lance corporal's mess tin was bubbling over a little flame. For him, how could the gobbets of blackening flesh, the earth well sotted with blood, with flesh, the eye under the duckboard, the pulpy bone be the only answer?'

Sentry duty was often tedious, as this drawing shows
Artist unknown

Rats by the Million

Vermin infested the trenches, as many soldiers and correspondents testified. Philip Gibbs waded through a water-filled trench which was 'alive with a multitude of swimming frogs'. The sides of the trench were covered with red slugs and horned beetles. Rats were among the worst horrors. They fed on corpses, grew as large as cats and sometimes attacked sleeping men.

Rats infested the battlefields in their tens of millions. Many soldiers were more horrified by these foul creatures than by anything else about frontline life. Two main types thrived on the Western Front – the

Soldiers faced the constant danger of being entombed by shell-bursts in the trenches. Here Corporal Sam Meekosha of 16th Territorial Battalion West Yorkshire Regiment leads a party digging out men buried during a furious bombardment on 19 November 1915. For this, as well as for courageous leadership, Meekosha was awarded the VC

E.A. Holloway

brown rat and the black rat, with the former much the bigger and more loathsome. Their favourite food was human flesh and in particular the eyes and liver. In this regard soldiers have told many appalling stories, and they are better left to the imagination. In the ideal breeding conditions provided on the Western Front, just one couple of rats produced nearly 900 offspring a year. They contaminated food and spread disease, including an infectious jaundice.

Soldiers shot rats, bayoneted, clubbed and poisoned them. The rats screamed when they were disturbed in their loathsome activities but only briefly desisted from them. Sometimes, however, they disappeared and veterans grew tense expecting an imminent bombardment. Among the experienced men it was accepted that rats sensed shell-fire a full 30 minutes before it began.

Lice

Lice were the great scourge of the trenches and the constant and inevitable companion of every soldier. The tiny insects flourished in the seams of dirty clothing where their eggs were incubated by body heat. They caused frenzied scratching. Widely known as 'chats' among the Australians, lice were pale fawn in colour and left blotchy red marks all over the body except on the head. They also created a distinctive, sour, stale smell. Captured German dugouts had a species of small red lice crawling over the walls and blankets.

Soldiers ran their finger-nails or a lighted candle along the seams of clothing to kill lice. Periodically, tunics and trousers were put through a delousing machine and underwear was sent to a laundry. However, a fair proportion of eggs remained in the clothes

and within a few hours of being put on a soldier's body heat would hatch them out. Lice transmitted an infectious disease known as trench fever. A common preliminary symptom was acute, shocking pain followed by high fever. Treatment called for up to 12 weeks off duty and the disease was a continual and heavy drain on manpower.

Nits infested the men's hair and every company had a barber to shave them to the skull, though many soldiers tried to keep a reasonable amount of hair.

Smells

The one major aspect of living and fighting on the Western Front which nobody can illustrate is the stench. The worst ingredient of the smell was the vile odour of putrefaction. In the frontline it permeated everything, even, according to some soldiers, the bread they ate. In addition, the latrines gave off a dreadful smell even in a well-ordered trench; so did the creosol and chloride of lime that was used to lessen the risk of infection and to drive away flies. Many trenches were hung with smoke from braziers, especially during the winter. For many soldiers the dominant smell, after putrefaction, was that of sweat. Virtually every action caused the men to sweat and until they got back to reserve they had no way of washing thoroughly. The feet gave off the worst smell and soldiers variously describe it as 'sickening', 'foul' and 'repulsive'.

Robert Graves gives one of the most graphic descriptions of the foul trench smell. It was 'compounded of stagnant mud, latrine buckets, chloride of lime, unburied and half-buried corpses, rotting sandbags, stale human sweat, fumes of cordite and lyddite. Sometimes it was sweetened by cigarette smoke and the scent of bacon

Despite the misery and discomfort, soldiers could still laugh when somebody slipped and fell in a water-logged trench. A French mishap of early 1916

Artist unknown

frying over wood fires, sometimes made sinister by the lingering odour of poison gas.'

'The stench was indescribably abominable', wrote a doctor after visiting a deep German dugout filled with dead and wounded. Another doctor said of his own RAP, 'There is blood everywhere; all other smells are drowned by its stench. Fumes from a coke brazier fill the place, and bits of clothing, equipment and dirty bloody dressings.'

More than 200,000 men were killed in the 30 square miles of the Somme battlefield and buried in shallow graves. Charles Carrington of the Warwickshire Regiment estimated the number of corpses at 7,000 to the square mile. 'Your nose told you where they lay thickest', he wrote.

Undoubtedly the worst horror for anybody new to the trenches was the corpses of men embedded amid the soil and sandbags.

'Every square yard of ground seemed to be layered with corpses,' wrote George Coppard. 'We curtained off protruding parts with a sandbag. A swollen right arm, with a German eagle tattooed on it, used to stick out and brush us as we squeezed by and once a head appeared which wasn't there an hour before.' Edmund Blunden reports that 'skulls appeared like mushrooms' from their shallow burial.

Water Supply

Some months of war passed before regular supplies of water to the trenches were organized. The delay was a result of the pervading notion that the trenches were only temporary, a mere aberration of war. It was decided, therefore, that the soldiers could easily exist on the contents of their water-bottles, which would be refilled as they returned from the frontline to reserve lines. However, the water-bottle supply was

By late 1917 army engineers had established water points in communication trenches, where company and platoon working parties filled the men's water bottles. The bottles came in two shapes, round and oblong, and both can be seen here

S. Ugo

far from adequate and the men depended on impure water which collected in shell-holes or other cavities. A standard, but unofficial, method of water collection developed in the trenches and was used for many months. A deep hole was dug in the trench floor, close to the parapet, and was lined with lightly filled sandbags as a filter. Rain-water seeped into the hole where it was collected, and it was then boiled for making tea or cocoa.

When it was realized that a proper, regular system was needed to supply the men in the forward trenches somebody thought of using the many empty 2-gallon petrol tins. When army transport men emptied petrol into their lorries, ambulances and tractors they just dropped the empties on the spot. Now, however, pioneers or infantry working parties collected them for recycling as water containers. All the cans were supposed to be 'fired' to burn any remaining petrol or oil before being filled with drinking water or hot tea, but countless cans were never fired and the petroleum contamination could last for many fillings. The frequent complaints that water reached the trenches 'tasting like petrol' were justified but throughout the war few water-only tins were supplied.

In mid-winter, when water supplies failed to arrive from the rear, the men used axes to smash lumps of ice from any puddle or pool in the trenches, the ice then being put into dixies. 'We used this ice for days to make tea,' an officer wrote, 'until one chap noticed a pair of boots sticking out of the ice, and discovered they were attached to a body.'

Any hot water that was available was reserved for officers so some soldiers saved a little of their tea for shaving.

Food

Each company going into the frontline took rations for three days, generally tins of bully beef, teeth-breaking biscuits and tins of jam. Some company or battalion quartermasters provided hard-boiled eggs or cold potatoes cooked in their skin, bread, fruit and condensed milk in tins. Not that all of these items were available at the same time.

Sometimes a fatigue party carried dixies full of hot stew or soup to the trenches, but a lot of this much-desired food did not arrive. It was spilled when the carriers slipped on the mud or when they were wounded by enemy gun-fire. Much depended on how close a field cooker could safely approach. The British army's field cooker had just two large vats, in which everything was prepared. Consequently, everything the men ate had several tastes, many of them unpleasant. Tea was rarely without the flavour of meat and vegetables.

The 'Tommy cooker', a pocket-sized stove operating on solidified alcohol, was the usual way of heating food and water but it was a slow process as the stove gave off only a weak heat. Soldiers dreamed up various ways of heating water. One of the most original was to soak a piece of rifle cleaning cloth in whale oil and light it in a tin. This rag was known officially as 'four-by-two' because a piece of flannel 4 in × 2 in was the regulation size required for pulling through the rifle barrel as it was cleaned. Known to the soldiers as 'forby', the oiled rag lasted long enough to heat a mess-tin full of water, Many a group of men clubbed together and bought a small primus stove for heating food and boiling water.

Army biscuit was so hard that it could be broken only by putting it on a hard surface and smashing it with a bayonet or shovel.

A British motor workshop at Albert. Army mechanics had set up their repair depot in a bombed house and were constantly busy. Vehicles often came to grief on the rough roads or were damaged by enemy fire. A sketch of July 1917

Artist unknown

The pieces could then be soaked in water, a softening process that might take days. Boiling in water was a faster process. When the sodden mass was covered in condensed milk it was tolerable to eat. After an initial smashing, biscuits could be boiled up with bully beef or sultanas or both, or with anything available, such as the odd potato or onion.

Despite the appalling conditions, many men retained a sense of humour in the trenches. Some stories of witticisms and wry humour spread from one unit to another and before long various battalions were claiming them as their own. One concerns the Welsh Division, though it would be difficult now to identify the unit from which it sprang:

Dai and Evan were chatting during trench breakfast after stand-down. 'Dai,' said Evan, 'which would you rather be killed in – a railway accident or an explosion?'

Dai thought about this for some minutes and then replied, 'I think I would rather be killed in a railway accident than an explosion.'

Evan pondered on this before he said, 'Well, why is that, Dai?'

Dai munched a piece of bread and jam

before he answered. 'Well, Evan, I think I would rather be killed in a railway accident because there you are, but if you are killed in an explosion, where the hell are you?'

Rum

The basic earthenware rum jar contained 1 gal, which was supposed to be enough for sixty-four men. The jars were marked with the black letters SRD, which some records show to mean Services Rum Diluted while other sources state Special Ration Distribution. The latter version could be the correct one since the first jars used during the Great War had been made at the turn of the century when temperance campaigners opposed alcohol for the troops. Special Ration Distribution was a camouflage label to fool them. More cynical meanings given to the abbreviation include 'Seldom Reaches Destination' and 'Soon Runs Dry'.

The notion that the rum issue produced drunkards is mistaken. In 1918 the entitlement for each British division – a paper strength of 20,000 – in the Western Front was 300 gals. This amount did not go far per man, except, according to the cynical rank and file, to the orderlies doling it out. They strongly believed that the orderlies, who were under the supervision of an officer, kept their thumb in the measuring beaker. This thumb of rum was considerable when added up for a platoon or company and was the orderlies' perk.

The French and German armies were issued daily with poor quality brandy and wine. The French called their brandy *gnole* and their wine *le pinard*.

Some divisional commanders kept their commands dry. One of them was General Pinney, GOC 33rd Division, who was a teetotaller. Rum could only be issued in emergencies, he ordered, but he failed to specify the nature of an emergency. Some humane battalion commanders within Pinney's division were ready to declare an emergency and authorize a rum issue.

Generally, rum was issued *after* an action, not before it, or in the trenches to give frozen men some warmth. The Australian army, as a policy, issued rum only after action.

CHAPTER 2

Dugouts

A scene in a British dugout at Christmas 1916. The Tommies have
found a practical use for a German steel helmet – they are
boiling a Christmas pudding in it. Snow is visible through a rear
window at the right

S. Begg

A small group of soldiers in a trench unpack Christmas fare which has reached them from home. It includes, to their great satisfaction, a plum pudding. A scene from just behind the frontline, in 1917.

Fortunino Matania

DUGOUTS

The first dugouts were literally dug out of the sides of trenches to create shelter from enemy shell-fire and from the weather. 'Dug-ins' might have been a more accurate description. Within a few months of the beginning of the war, any deep shelter, such as the cellar of a house or the crypt of a church, was called a dugout. A shell-hole or a mine crater or just any hole in the ground was *not* a dugout; to classify in military parlance as a dugout overhead shelter was necessary. Nor was a 'funk' hole a dugout. A 'funk' hole was merely a niche carved into a trench wall where a soldier could escape from the traffic of the trench when he was not actively on duty and where he had a certain amount of protection from shrapnel, though not from the shards of shells exploding in the trenches or behind them. Many commanders banned 'funk' holes after losing men from suffocation when the soil collapsed.

A dugout might be big enough for only a few men or it might hold ten or more. The 1911 edition of the *Manual of Field Engineering*, which was in use for much of the war, recommended square-cut recesses between 2 ft and 4 ft 6 in wide, roofed with boards, corrugated iron or brushwood and then covered with a minimum of 9 in of earth. This protection was considered adequate against shrapnel balls, shell splinters and grenade bursts. The *Manual* advised that numerous shelters of this type were better than a few elaborate ones.

The really big underground shelters were known as mine dugouts. The Catacombs, dug out by the Australians behind Messines in 1917, could hold two battalions of soldiers at a time. Many dugouts behind the trenches accommodated 200 to 500 men in what they would have regarded as reasonable comfort.

We generally apply the label of dugouts to the Germans' deep, concrete-lined and well equipped underground shelters but they were more like underground barracks. From 1915, the remarkably well developed German positions, notably on the Somme front, reflected their strategic advantage. They were on enemy soil, the Germans held the initiative and they could afford to settle down in their dugouts. Hence, most had electricity, drainage, sewerage system, piped water, a telephone system and many were heated. The soldiers could lie down on mattresses resting on beds made of sacking stretched over wooden frames, and because of deep overhead cover – 30 to 40 ft of it – they were safe even during heavy shell-fire. In these positions they felt little strain or tension and when an alarm sounded and they ran out to man the trenches they were dry and rested. Officers' quarters had carpets on the wooden floors. It was said that some dugouts at Le Sars, Somme, were fitted with window-shaped mirrors which gave the illusion of being in above ground accommodation.

Some dugouts were ingeniously con-

This elaborate position in Flanders was a dugout and machine-gun emplacement combined. On the left are the sleeping quarters. The gun is in the background near the boxes of bullets. The bottle on the table contains the hypo solution for soaking the respirators. The overhead cover is shallow and a heavy shell would have pulped this dugout

Drawn by an officer at the front

structed, with a concealed access leading to a sharply sloping stepped half-gallery; this is the mining term for a narrow shaft. Others were reached by a ladder descending through a half-gallery in the shape of a well. The first British troops who captured some of the elaborate German 'dugouts' were amazed at their comfort. Officers who heard about these places made special trips to inspect them and were also astounded, especially by those under the heights of Thiepval.

At St Pierre Divion and Beaumont Hamel the German dugouts extended for nearly a mile beneath Y Ravine. According to a British officer who inspected them, the corridors were beautifully built of wood and

fitted with every convenience including electric light. He found a well equipped surgery and a telephone exchange, together with the big bell from Beaumont Hamel church which the Germans used for sounding the gas alarm. The officers' mess had large mirrors on the walls and Japanese lanterns shading the electric lamps.

The French and British High Commands were not prepared to settle down in the way the Germans did. To push the Germans out they had to move forward and there was little sense, as the Allied generals saw it, in preparing permanent, comfortable dugouts.

Nevertheless, some British dugouts had a certain kind of crude luxury, as officers' servants vied with one another to improve their respective officer's shelter. One such shelter, near Bois Grenier, had a sliding glass window onto the trench, a pull-down washstand, folding table and armchair with footstool. Such comfort was only possible when a unit was in the line for some time, as many were during March and April 1915. Some officers put mascots at the door of their dugouts. The war correspondent Philip Gibbs noticed a woman's face carved in chalk, the name of a girl written in pebbles and a portrait of King George V in a frame of withered flowers.

In breastworks (q.v.) a dugout was not dug at all, but a space was left for a shelter as the breastworks were built and it was then roofed. In trenches, a dugout was created by pick and shovel work into the trench side, often at trench floor level, but sometimes several steps below that level. The resulting hole was given roof supports of logs or dressed timber and the walls were revetted with timber or filled sandbags.

Deep enough for men to stand upright, they were furnished with built-in bunks or beds made of wire netting stretched over wooden frames, together with a few rough chairs made from boxes. Blankets or hessian screened off the entrance, mostly to keep out draughts but also as a protection against poison gas and to prevent tell-tale light from showing at night. Since the floors of dugouts were always wet they were covered with duckboards. The air was fetid from candle and tobacco smoke, from damp and sweat, and any form of ventilation was primitive. When it could be arranged, a dugout was provided with a brazier for warmth and cooking. The fumes from braziers caused many fatalities in inadequately ventilated dugouts.

Frontline dugouts generally served as pla-

A dugout originally made by the French but taken over by the British. It has a hinged door and strong head cover

Artist unknown

toon or company headquarters and provided sleeping accommodation for the officers. Officers' servants were usually lucky enough to be able to curl up on the floor of a dugout. Depending on the fastidiousness of its occupants and the availability of supplies, a dugout might have a gramophone, bookshelves, a cover for the table and a lamp rather than a candle. Some dugouts were surprisingly comfortable, others were hideously cramped and uncomfortable. In either case, the occupants were better off than in the open trenches.

By 1916 prefabricated materials were being used in dugout construction and prob-

This is said to be a 'typical trench dugout' of 1915. A telegraphist is handing the company commander a message just received. The other officer is making cocoa over a spirit stove, near which is a Very flare pistol. Over this dugout is a roof of branches, boards and debris, all covered with about 1 ft of earth. This was sufficient protection against shrapnel and shell splinters but not a direct hit

D. McPherson

A frontline dugout drawn as a battalion Christmas card in 1916. If the drawing was taken from life it was obviously a quiet period

Two parts of a Western Front dugout on a company front. On the left an officer uses a field telephone and to the right is the officers' mess. There is limited sleeping accommodation but not all the officers would be asleep at one time

A. Forestier

ably chief among them were the curved corrugated iron sheets known as 'elephants'. Their main use was to provide arches of various lengths. The 'small elephant' was a strip 3 ft 9 in high, 5 ft wide and 12 ft 9 in long. The 'big elephant' strip was an arch 6 ft 5 in high and 2 ft 9 in deep and twenty-one sections could be bolted together to give a 'large elephant shelter' 17 ft 9 in long and 9 ft wide. The prefab 'elephants' were dug into the earth to form the roof of chamber or dugout.

By 1916 dugout frames were increasingly made well behind the lines by engineer and pioneer units or were contracted out to local workshops. They were sent to the trenches in kit form and assembled by pioneers or infantry working parties.

Contemporary literature of the war is full of references to dugouts and they played a large part in the social and military life of the trenches. A dugout housed company headquarters from where the officer in command, usually a captain, controlled the routine of his sector, though the busiest man was generally the company sergeant-major.

Effectively, he was the NCO on whom trench discipline rested. People were constantly pushing past the blanket or hessian screen on some errand or another. Sometimes, a platoon commander on reaching the trenches was lucky enough to find a smaller dugout in which he could set up his own small HQ.

By the winter of 1917–18, dugouts, especially those for battalion HQ, were much more complex than the crowded single-chamber of earlier years. Even the positioning was different, the entrance to the dugout complex being set into the side of a communication trench so that it was not directly in the line of fire from enemy guns. The complex might have a central corridor of more than 100 ft, with three sets of stairways linking it to the surface in the communication trench.

At the foot of each stairway was a mini-complex. One comprised the commanding officer's office, a 'room' containing his bed and perhaps two others, the officers' mess and a kitchen. The second section consisted of a general office, the signals room and a small room with beds for the duty officers. The third section contained sleeping accommodation for about thirty NCOs and men. Great variations existed from one such dugout complex to another because of earth composition, building materials available, the ingenuity of the engineers responsible and requirements specified by brigade HQ, which was the arbiter of such constructions.

In France, virtually every house had a cellar and when the troops took over a wrecked village they turned the cellars into dugouts, or more correctly in the terminology of the time, mine dugouts. Some were 30 ft deep and 20 ft was not uncommon. Almost invariably, these shelters were given

The term dugout does not do justice to this elaborately constructed German underground shelter. Together with similar corridors it was found at Y Ravine, Beaumont Hamel during the battle of the Ancre towards the end of 1916. The corridors were up to 40 ft deep and extended for nearly a mile. Along the wall sets of light railway line are fastened. The door on the extreme right led to the doctors' quarters and telephone exchange. The big bell is from Beaumont Hamel church, and the Germans used it for sounding the gas alarm. The officers' mess is at the far end. Three dead Germans were found

S. Begg

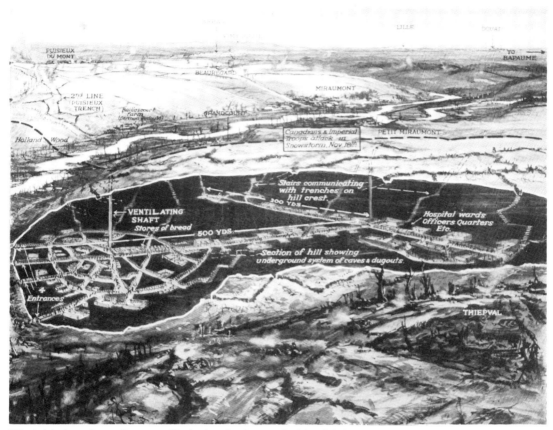

This sketch shows the position, near Albert, where the Germans had dug their immense underground shelters

D. McPherson

a second or third exit in case one should be blocked during bombardment. Church crypts made excellent dugouts and some were big enough to be turned into protected supply dumps, as in Zonnebeke church, Ypres. The crypt of a church at Mont St Quentin is said to have been reached by forty-seven steps. The Germans were there first and they had made it very comfortable.

Capturing German trench dugouts was a dangerous procedure and British and Empire soldiers soon learned not to enter them. Instead, they threw in some grenades and after the explosion shouted to the occupants to come out. Even then some Germans were likely to remain in a dugout so a sentry was posted at the entrance, to kill or capture any enemy who ventured out. There is little evidence to show that German troops were entombed by shell-fire in their powerful dugouts, but many British and Commonwealth soldiers died in this way. Their much weaker dugouts could not withstand a hurricane bombardment.

The shell feared most by British and Empire troops was the 150 mm field howitzer shell, always known to the British as 'the 5.9'. This penetrated several feet before exploding and shelters at least 10 ft deep were needed as protection.

CHAPTER 3

No Man's Land; Wiring;
Flame-throwers

As a German flare explodes a member of a British wiring party hits
the ground, while his comrades freeze and hope that the enemy
does not see them

Artist unknown

Rival reconnaissance patrols clash in No Man's Land in April 1917. A flare has gone up and both patrols jump
into a shell-hole. If any of the men had fired his weapon a hail of fire would have swept the field so they fought it
out with bayonet and rifle butt

S. Eduardo

NO MAN'S LAND

No Man's Land is an interesting and evocative term. Both sides quickly came to use it from the spring of 1915, and in doing so they were tacitly admitting the impossibility of mastering the ground. It was indeed nobody's territory, since it was that part of the front which lay between the opposing trenches. Some official issue trench maps show that in places it was a mere 8 yd across. Elsewhere it was as much as 500 yd, but the more usual distance was 150 yd in French and Belgian Flanders and 200 yd elsewhere. The narrowest No Man's Land was only a few yards. At La Boiselle some soldiers claimed that they were so close to the enemy that they could stick their bayonets in the German sandbags. I can find no evidence that they actually tried it! Sometimes No Man's Land was a crater blown by a mine, with opposing soldiers holding the lip on either side of the crater.

In many places, at various times, the combatants were separated only by the width of a barricade in the same trench. The Australians at Bullecourt in April and again in May 1917 had this dangerous experience, as did the British at Bellewarde in 1915.

The barbed-wire defences erected by both sides were in No Man's Land. Also debris, rubble, smashed equipment and bodies littered those stretches of No Man's Land where fighting had taken place before the front had become defined and set.

No Man's Land was far from devoid of human life. Out there, soldiers from both sides crouched in listening posts, while scouts crawled out, even during daylight, to spy on the enemy's defences. It was at night, however, that No Man's Land became busy. Then reconnaissance patrols, fighting patrols and raiding companies ventured out from their lines. A recce patrol consisted of only a few men, under an NCO or officer, and its task was to bring back information about enemy wire, positions and troop movements. All recce patrols were under strict orders not to pick a fight, and to shoot only if that became necessary in order to escape after being discovered. Such patrols were tense and risky. Some brave and enterprising parties – or perhaps foolhardy ones – managed to crawl to the very edge of an enemy trench and spend a few minutes listening and peering in. For a German-speaking British officer or soldier even a snatch of overheard conversation could yield valuable information. It might reveal that the front at that point was being held by Bavarians, Wurttembergers or Saxons and as some enemy troops were regarded as being so inferior to others the information could decide a British general to launch an attack. Other valuable snippets of conversation might indicate that the enemy was short of ammunition or that a trench relief was expected at a certain time.

The men who enjoyed the excitement and danger of recce work went to lengths to do their job. For them the more debris in No Man's Land the better, since it could provide cover from view and sometimes from fire. I know of cases where a scout dragged the corpse of one of his own side into a shell-hole and then resumed the prone position of the dead man – and maintained it throughout the hours of daylight in order to observe movement in the enemy lines. He had to take up the exact sprawl of the corpse, no matter how uncomfortable, so that the suspicions of German observers and snipers was not aroused. Even then he ran a risk since a sniper might put a bullet into a corpse just to make sure it really was a corpse.

Whenever a patrol went out it was given a precise position for its return, since it was often quite different from the point of departure. Along the relevant part of the Allied line sub-units were warned that an 'own' patrol would be coming in at a particular place. For further safety, everybody was told the password of the operation. Even so, men on patrol regarded their return as one of the most dangerous periods of their adventure. Tense, trigger-happy sentries often fired at any movement and caused many British casualties. On one occasion an Australian sentry killed two of his mates, returning one behind the other, with a single shot.

Perhaps the most frightening moment of all came when the defenders fired a flare to illuminate the battlefield. Soldiers were taught to freeze when this happened, to remain absolutely motionless until the flare dropped to earth and died. A pistol flare remained bright for 10 to 15 seconds but it seemed an eternity to the men lying under it. Sometimes the defenders swept No Man's Land with machine-gun fire while the

Two British soldiers on reconnaissance patrol in No Man's Land, armed only with revolvers, throw themselves face down as a brilliant flare arcs above them. This type of flare lasted for 15 seconds, a lifetime for the scouts

A. Forestier

The Ulster Division goes over the top into No Man's Land in the battle of the Somme, 1 July 1916. They fought valiantly and suffered grievously

J. P. Beadle

flare lasted, whether or not they were sure of a target.

The Germans also used what the British called a 'light-shell rocket'. Suspended from a small parachute, the flare blazed brightly for about a minute. Patrols and working parties caught under such an intense flare said that it was like lying out in sunshine. Fortunately, the rockets showed little light for the first half of their flight and this gave soldiers trapped in No Man's Land just enough time to throw themselves face down. Here they had to lie absolutely motionless while the flare lasted and be ready for a second or third one to be fired if the watching enemy was still suspicious.

Sometimes opposing patrols stumbled across each other and a shoot-out would result or, just as frequently, both patrols would dive for cover and crawl away. There were even times when, for the sake of survival, opposing patrols turned away from

each other and went about their business unmolested.

Only the hardiest and most adventurous of men really found patrolling exciting. Most returned from a patrol physically exhausted and emotionally and mentally drained. Several confessed that they were 'changed men' after a patrol.

Another nocturnal activity in No Man's Land was the laying of white tapes in readiness for an infantry attack. This was usually the responsibility of the battalion intelligence officer (IO). With his helpers, the IO was required to set out tapes indicating the jumping-off line for the assault, the edge of each battalion's front and the direction of the enemy front to be attacked. It was imperative that the tape laying be carried out without arousing the enemy's suspicions. Sometimes an enterprising intelligence or scout officer placed lanterns, with a thin beam of light shining only towards his own lines, to guide the troops on an especially dark night.

Many of these intrepid officers had adventures in No Man's Land while carrying out their duty. One of them was Captain Albert Jacka, VC, MC, of the 14th Australian Battalion, who prepared the tapes before the Australian attack on the Hindenburg Line at Bullecourt in April 1917. In the gloom, Jacka spotted a German officer and his orderly who were also on patrol and seemed about to discover the giveaway tapes. After a kicking, punching fight Jacka captured the Germans and dragged them into the Australian lines. The German officer, a Wurttemberger, complained to Jacka's colonel that he had been treated roughly, but he was alive only because as a corpse he would have been more difficult to remove from No Man's Land.

WIRING

Wiring in No Man's Land was a job for skilled soldiers and was a dreaded task. Much wire was erected before the armies were fully in position and was carried out with few casualties. After this period it was a nocturnal activity, with the men on tenterhooks as they anticipated enemy flares and machine-guns firing. Wiring was a dangerous business where No Man's Land was narrow. First of all the 6 ft steel pickets, rolls of wire and the mallets had to be carried to the position selected and here the men were shown where to set up the wire. In charge were NCOs, perhaps from pioneer or engineer units, who had previously reconnoitred the area. There followed the labour of driving or winding in the pickets, often with muffled mallets, and then the difficult task of attaching the wire. When fastened to the pickets, the wire was pulled out to make a single 'apron', on one side of the line of pickets, or a 'double apron', on both sides. Such a barrier was virtually impassable and assault infantry had to cut a path with wire-cutters or blow a gap with a Bangalore torpedo. This was a long pipe filled with explosive and exploded under the wire by lighting a fuse. Alternatively, the artillery could be asked to destroy wire with high explosive shells but such a bombardment was often ineffectual.

The wire that could be laid most rapidly was concertina wire, which was simply pulled out from a large circular coil to a length of up to 25 yd.

On several recorded occasions, wiring parties from both sides found themselves at work within yards of each other – and completely ignoring the embarrassing situation, carried on with feverish speed and finished their job. When one side left, so did the other. Whoever reached the safety of their trenches first, opened fire.

Tactically, wire had two purposes. It was placed far enough from the trenches to prevent the enemy from approaching close enough to lob grenades in. Other entanglements were set up 50 to 100 yd from the trench and so laid out as to channel attacking infantry into machine-gun fire. Frequently, wire was placed out of sight or partly out of sight in woods, hollows or ditches, where it would surprise the enemy.

Men of a British wiring party in the Ypres Salient freeze as they are caught in the open by an enemy flare, hoping that their immobility will save them. Notice the muffled mallet in the upright soldier's hand. The posts, rather than steel pickets, show this to be a 1914–15 drawing

Artist unknown

FLAME-THROWERS

During 1915, first the French and then the British discovered that No Man's Land concealed another menace – German troops using *Flammenwerfers* or flame-throwers. At Hooge, Ypres, the British troops first subjected to these weapons spoke of 'liquid fire' and this is what the great and terrifying gouts of flame must have looked like.

The Germans used three types of flame-thrower – the *Grossflammenwerfer* or *Gross*; the *Kleinflammenwerfer* or *Klein* and, in 1917, the *Wex*, a lightweight appara-

A German soldier, using a *Kleinflammenwerfer*, sprays a mixture of burning oil and petrol onto British trenches at Hooge, Ypres. The Tommies called it 'liquid fire'. The Germans had some initial success with this terror weapon but the Allied soldiers soon lost their fear of it

A. Forestier

tus. The *Gross*, an offensive–defensive weapon, was built into the trench system. It had a range of 45 yd and could squirt flame for a minute. It was effective when the opposing trenches were close together and the flame could leap No Man's Land. The backpack *Klein* had a range of 25 yd and could be operated from No Man's Land. The *Wex* was considered 'advanced' because it could be automatically ignited while the others were ignited by a torch. All used an oil mixture which burned for several minutes when it settled on a target. While few casualties were caused by the flame-throwers they were frightening weapons and the Germans made 653 attacks with them. Soldiers using them from No Man's Land had a short life expectancy since scores of rifles and light machine-guns were fired at them.

The British experimented with flame-throwers, found them inefficient and as a result abandoned totally the idea of using portable short-range jets. In mid-1916 monster flame-throwing machines were tried. This involved the task of digging or tunnelling into No Man's Land and preparing a special chamber. Into this, a 2-ton thrower was dragged piece by piece, followed by containers of oil and cylinders of compressed air. Four contraptions were put together only 60 yd from the German line, giving the flame a lethal zone of up to another 30 yd. Enemy shell-fire destroyed two machines but on 1 July the other two were ignited and frightening streams of fire gushed over the German lines. They drove the enemy from a short length of trench and killed a few soldiers, without gaining the slightest tactical advantage. With this failure, flame-throwers were abandoned.

CHAPTER 4

Artillery

The sole surviving member of a gun team continues to serve his 18-pounder. This fine drawing exemplifies the courage of British gunners during the fierce fighting of August–September 1914, at Mons, Le Cateau and Néry. The artist gave this creation the title 'Went the day well? We died and never knew.' In these two months six members of the Royal Field Artillery and two of the Royal Horse Artillery won the Victoria Cross

Christopher Clark

Just behind the gun positions, gunners unload an artillery reserve shell wagon in an effort to satisfy the guns'
insatiable appetite. A scene on the Somme in November 1917

R. Caton Woodville

ARTILLERY

For soldiers, the word 'gun' means an artillery piece. A man who referred to his personal weapon, the Lee Enfield, as a gun would have been reprimanded by any instructor or NCO. This was his rifle, he would be told, sharply, unless he happened to be unlawfully using a 12-bore shotgun. Machine-guns, whether the medium Vickers or the light Lewis, also were never simply called 'guns', but referred to by their manufacturers or inventor's name. Yet again, a mortar was not, in army terminology, a gun, but a howitzer, which in use is a type of mortar, *is* a gun.

The guns gave the Great War on the Western Front the sound and fury, the destruction and the horror, that are associated with this conflict. As the war became increasingly static after the 1914 battles, so the production of guns increased. Even the generals who failed to appreciate the significance of machine-guns and mortars understood the importance of guns. The demand for more and more shells for the guns was incessant but for long periods, in the British and French armies, they had to be rationed, so great was the consumption.

The types of guns and shells used depended on the effect wanted. High explosive shells killed many men but only incidentally; they were intended to destroy enemy trenches and fortifications, buildings and dumps, roads and transport – and enemy guns. Shrapnel shells, however, were fired against infantry and cavalry, especially when they were attacking or in the open. British 13- and 18-lb shrapnel shells were set to detonate at a height of 16 ft above the ground. This was considered the optimum killing height, with the steel balls spewing from the shell casing at great velocity. A properly directed shrapnel barrage could break up an infantry attack, even without the help of machine-guns.

The type of barrage also varied. When infantry attacked in large numbers they generally did so behind a creeping barrage, a protective curtain of fire from their own guns. Just how close they were to the bursting shells depended on the degree of nerve which senior officers expected of their men. Thirty yards was commonplace for Australians in 1917 and 1918. This was dangerously close, but it meant that the attacking Diggers were upon the enemy before they had pulled themselves together from the shock of the barrage.

A box barrage was laid down around a target area to prevent the enemy command from sending in reinforcements. However, during even the heaviest of box barrages determined men of all armies managed to get through the bursting shells to support their comrades, who would soon have to repel infantry attackers.

A pin-point barrage was used to wipe out a troublesome machine-gun nest or even a lone but deadly sniper.

Another type of fire was the searching barrage, by which artillery batteries on one side would 'search' areas behind enemy lines for opposing batteries, headquarters, wagon lines and dumps. While this was sometimes speculative shelling, it often followed reports from aerial observers or spies. By hitting an ammunition dump gunners struck a devastating blow against the enemy.

A counter-battery barrage was targeted wholly against the enemy's guns. With good observation and a system of flash-spotting, surveying and sound-ranging it was possible to fix the position of enemy batteries, even well concealed ones, and destroy them before they had time to limber-up and move to another location. The German artillery, which had the advantage of higher ground for the greater part of the war, wrought great destruction among the British and Empire batteries.

Yet another type of barrage, using high explosive howitzer shells exclusively, was designed to cut enemy barbed wire. The job was never satisfactorily done and many soldiers complained that the shell-fire merely made the wire more difficult to get through.

Finally, the guns were used to fire smoke and gas shells, usually in conjunction with a high explosive bombardment.

The intensity of barrages, for the gunners delivering them, was 'light', 'moderate' or 'heavy'. A 'light' barrage amounted to six or seven shells every ten minutes on an infantry company's front trench. A 'moderate' pounding was thirty shells a minute and a 'heavy' one, fifty to sixty shells a minute. A barrage would not dwell for long on any one target if infantry were attacking behind it, but a bombardment intended to demoralize

From a dangerously exposed advanced observation post – the ubiquitous OP – officers note the effect of British artillery fire and report to the batteries

Fortunino Matania

Gun teams of the Royal Field Artillery advance in November 1917. A bridge is struck by a German shell just as a gun is crossing it.

R. Caton Woodville

soldiers and pulverize their defences could last from a few hours to two or three weeks.

British and French infantry suffered severely from drop-shorts fired by their own guns. The gunners blamed defects in the shells and propellant charges, faulty fuses and worn gun barrels. Sometimes they told angry infantry officers that they had given inaccurate information about where they wanted shells to pitch. Whatever the reasons or excuses given by the gunners, the infantry considered drop-shorts to be inexcusable.

According to one French general, 75,000 French soldiers were killed by their own guns. There is no way in which he could produce any figure and claim it to be accurate, but since almost every soldier who wrote about the war complained of drop-shorts the number of 'own casualties' was no doubt high. The Australian official historian, C.E.W. Bean, records several cases of

British or Australian batteries firing on their own men by mistake.

German soldiers also complained about under-shooting by their guns. Their 49th Field Artillery Regiment, a persistent offender, became bitterly known among the infantry as the '48½ regiment'.

The German army began the war with a large number of heavy howitzers, which lobbed shells into the enemy's defences and caused fearful destruction. The British and French had traditionally opted for field guns. The British had 13- and 18-pounders, while the French had their famous 75 mm. Quite soon, both sides acquired many more guns of the type favoured by their adversaries. By mid-1916 the Royal Artillery was using many hundreds of 6-in, 8-in and 9.2-in howitzers, always known as 'hows' by the gunners. The 9.2-in howitzer was a massive beast and even the 6-in weighed 26 cwt and was cumbersome in the mud.

A British battery crosses a quagmire during the battle of Broodseinde, Ypres, October 1917. The artist says, 'The
ground is hopeless and beyond the powers of six-horse teams. Ten for each gun are needed, perhaps twelve.
When a gun slips into a shellhole and cannot be hauled out by the horses it must be dug out under shellfire'

Wallace Coop

In planning the Somme offensive for July 1916, the British and French High Commands depended on a massive, lengthy artillery barrage to destroy all German resistance. All the evidence of previous similar attacks showed that this would not happen. Nevertheless, the British and French marshalled more than 1,300 heavy guns – quite apart from lighter field guns – and 2,000,000 shells. Most of the shells were fired within seven days and after this colossal bombardment most of the officers involved were confident that no German could be left alive in the enemy trenches. As

British casualties show, they were mistaken.

During the first two weeks of Third Ypres, July 1917, the British, Australian and Canadian guns fired 4,283,550 shells. This was a year's output for 55,000 munitions workers. The figure for the entire war was 170 million. In addition, many millions of bombs were fired from mortars. The total weight of metal thrown at the enemy was 5,000,000 tons.

For all its destructive power, artillery was not decisive in any battle until 1918. The German High Command had experimented with many systems of gun-fire, and for the attempt to break through the Allied lines in March 1918 the generals decided on a hurricane bombardment. Abandoning the steady, day-after-day drenching of the enemy position with high explosive shells, the German artillery hit selected Allied targets with a mixture of high explosive, gas and smoke shells. In five hours, the German attack caused complete confusion and disorganization in the British lines, followed by a near-rout in some parts of the line.

A single shell exploding close by was frightening, a brief bombardment was terrifying and sustained shell-fire was demoralizing. This is how one soldier described the tumult of a barrage:

A diabolical uproar surrounds us. We are conscious of a sustained crescendo, an incessant multiplication of the universal frenzy; a hurricane of hoarse and hollow banging of raging clamour, of piercing and beast-like screams, fastens furiously with tatters of smoke upon the earth where we are buried up to our necks, and the wind of the shells seems to set it heaving and pitching.

Men subjected to the continual or repeated

An 18-pounder gun battery in action in the summer of 1915. An order has arrived by telephone and a soldier calls it to the officer in command. He unfolds his map, quickly studies it and shouts, 'Tell the observer we will fire on X!' Obviously, the area has not been subjected to counter-battery fire because the houses are only lightly damaged. The drawing repays study

Fortunino Matania

strain of shell-fire gradually broke down and many moaned and whimpered. The strain was never worse than during the fighting at Verdun in 1916 when the incessant din and trembling of the earth reduced French and German soldiers to gibbering, tearful wrecks. When one side or the other raided the other's positions after a bombardment they found their enemy so numbed that they were incapable of fighting. Between them, the two sides fired 40 million shells into the Verdun battlefield between February and June 1916.

'Shell-shock', the term which was widely used to describe the traumatic effect of gun-fire on men's nerves, was apt enough. It is hardly surprising that many men went mad.

Right: Taking rations to the
trenches, near Lihons,
October 1916
> *François Flameng*

Below: In the trenches of
Notre-Dame-de-Lorette
after a downpour, June
1915
> *François Flameng*

Overleaf
Main picture: French troops
advance across flooded
ground towards Bixschoote,
Flanders, on 31 July 1917.
A systematic, coordinated
assault was impossible in
such a mire
> *Artist unknown*

Inset: A French soldier of
1915 carries his wounded
officer out of further danger.
The artist called his painting
'Two Heroes'
> *Georges Scott*

Spad fighter plane on patrol over the trenches in January 1918

François Flameng

CHAPTER 5

Raids; Patrols; Attacks; Snipers

French soldiers exultantly capture a key German position at
Verdun on 15 December 1916. In six months of fighting the French
and Germans each lost 500,000 men. Forty million shells were fired
Lucien Jonas

A classic reconnaissance patrol, with an officer and two men, somewhere in the Ypres Salient, in the winter of
1915–16. This patrol's main mission was to make contact with a unit dislodged during a bombardment

S. Ugo

RAIDS

Trench raids began within a few months of the start of the war and were still being made in September 1918. They had three main purposes: one was to maintain an aggressive spirit in the men, another to capture prisoners for interrogation and unit identification and the third to 'put some ginger into Jerry', as some generals expressed it. That is, the Germans had to be kept on edge and deprived of sleep. No matter what the main objective of a raid might be it was always necessary to cause as much damage as possible.

The minimum strength for a trench raid was a platoon of roughly thirty men, but a half company of sixty men or an entire company was more usual. The leader was generally a captain but sometimes a major. The men practised a raid on dummy trenches – at least from 1916 on – and prepared for the raid itself to a strict routine. Badges and regimental buttons were usually removed to avoid giving the enemy information about the unit involved and uniforms were fastened with safety pins. Identity discs were retained because no unit name or number was shown on them but pay-books and all letters and documents were left behind.

Steel helmets, which were a hindrance to rapid movement and might make a noise if they dropped off during the approach, were often discarded in favour of woollen caps. Faces were blackened or mud-smeared.

Equipment was reduced to a minimum, little more than basic webbing to hold ammunition pouches and the water-bottle. The rifle and bayonets were essential for some members of a raiding party but after experience of trench raids many soldiers relied more on clubs, which were of many kinds. A strip of lead tightly worked around the end of a stout stick made a lethal bone cruncher. Various daggers and knives were also developed. However, from late 1915 the main attacking weapon was the grenade. Bombers, or grenadiers, were the basis of the raiding party. Leaping into an enemy trench, or sometimes by running along the parapet, the bombers raced from traverse to traverse, bombing as they went. The bayonet men killed the enemy soldiers who survived the bombing. Another technique was for two bayonet men to lead the way along a trench while the bombers threw from behind them. The raid leader, with his runner, followed the first bombers. Behind them were bomb carriers, replacement throwers and bayonet men. At the tail of the party, an NCO and a few men faced rearwards against counter-attack from that position.

One famous Canadian raider of D Company, 50th Battalion, known as 'Corporal Tom', had an incredible speciality. On night raiding parties he took a strong cord snare which he flung around the neck of some unsuspecting German and hauled him choking out of a trench to force him back to HQ for identification and questioning.

As soon as a prisoner or two were captured they were bundled out of the trench by men already detailed for the job and hustled back to friendly lines. The time allotted for a raid was precise, possibly 15 minutes in the enemy's trenches, perhaps 5 minutes. If the raiders stayed too long the defenders had time to rush in reinforcements, then a pitched battle would result. This had to be avoided since the intention was not to occupy enemy trenches, as with an attack, but to create havoc in them and get out. Getting their own wounded back was always a great problem for raiders but many a raid took place without serious wounds to any of its members.

Raids were also made to destroy enemy strongpoints, especially machine-gun posts. This aim was often achieved but the Germans quickly re-established such posts with a fresh gun and crew.

A raid to capture prisoners for identification and interrogation. Some British troops are still bombing enemy trenches, while others hurry their prisoners to the rear

R. Caton Woodville

PATROLS

Irish troops storm German positions at Guillemont, Somme, in September 1916. A lance-corporal bayoneted three of the enemy in rapid succession yet was himself untouched, while a German officer killed one Irish soldier and wounded two with his pistol before being overpowered. Philip Gibbs, the war correspondent, described the Irish attack as 'a human avalanche'

A. Forestier

The British and Empire armies trained their soldiers in three types of patrol: fighting, reconnaissance and standing patrols.

The fighting patrol generally consisted of a platoon up to a maximum of a company and its purpose was straightforward – to look for trouble and inflict loss and damage upon the enemy. A platoon was normally commanded by just one officer but when it was detailed for duty as a fighting patrol two officers would often accompany it, in case one should be killed or disabled. The men were fully armed but they wore minimum equipment so that they could move fast. The patrol was often given a specific objective, such as a certain length of enemy trench or a machine-gun post, but sometimes its commander was permitted to deviate from his original orders should he see a better target. The leader of a raid had no such licence. Generally, a fighting patrol had a time limit so that troops manning the trenches where the patrol was to return had a good idea of the time to expect it.

A reconnaissance patrol consisted of only a few men, perhaps an officer with an NCO and one man, though many a recce patrol was led by an experienced sergeant or corporal. Such a patrol was under strict orders not to fight, except in self-defence should it be attacked. Its task was to scout and bring back information.

All soldiers, from the private in the trenches to the general at HQ, were curious to know about the enemy troops on a given front. Depending on where in Germany or Austria they came from, it was possible to estimate the probable extent of opposition. Some German divisions were so placid that they would do almost anything to avoid a fight while others seemed eager for combat. The Saxons were said to be easygoing, Silesians

A company prepares for a night raid in July 1917 starting from an old disused trench. Two officers are using a captured German flashlight-box for signalling, while the raid leader studies his map. Note the canvas buckets for carrying grenades and the Lewis gun leaning against the trench

R. Caton Woodville

A French raiding party, attacking from the rear, surprises the German defenders in October 1915. The incident took place in the Vosges forest

J. Simont

conscientious but not fire-eaters, the Bavarians stout-hearted and the Prussians tough. On innumerable occasions when No Man's Land was narrow, the Germans would shout that they weren't looking for trouble. Some even put up placards carrying the word 'Peace' or 'Pax' or 'Paix'. A British officer reported that a German bellowed, 'Hold your fire! The Prussians will be here next week. They'll give you a fight!'

Generally, the recce patrol leader was given no time limit since he might have to spend hours simply lying and watching. All members of a recce patrol were lightly armed and sometimes the only weapons carried were revolvers. Officers choosing men for a recce patrol were careful not to include those known to be aggressive and impulsive.

A standing patrol was used less frequently than the others. It usually consisted of a half company, possibly a full company, and the task of its leaders was to establish the patrol at a certain specific point and stay there for a predetermined length of time. For instance, a standing patrol might be sent to a road junction to stop the enemy from passing through it so that they would not stumble upon engineers preparing a new defensive position. A standing patrol, which was well armed and carried reserve ammunition, moved quickly and directly to its objective, held the position against whatever attacks might eventuate and withdrew at the time ordered. It differed from a 'fixed post' in only one way – the garrison of a 'fixed post' fought to the last man.

ATTACKS

An attack was on a much larger scale than a raid but fell far short of an offensive, which involved an entire front, corps and armies. A division, which has a nominal strength of 20,000 men, might make the attack. If two or three divisions were involved the operation became a corps attack. On this scale the operation was more complex than a raid and involved extensive preparations. For instance, artillery was generally required to soften up the enemy defences before the infantry advanced. Close liaison and co-operation among the four brigades of a division was essential and this involved staff work. An attack by a division or larger formation was intended not only to break the enemy line but to hold any positions taken. This inevitably meant sustained fighting so preparations had to be made to supply the forward troops with ammunition, grenades, food and water and other needs.

Some brigades and divisions went to great lengths to plan their assaults by organizing what became known as 'white tape rehearsals'. The Canadians and Australians placed much stress on dummy runs from 1917 on. Miles of white and coloured tape were laid out over the ground representing the proposed jumping off positions and those of the enemy during the various stages of the advance. Tapes indicated pillboxes, barbed wire entanglements, suspected mine positions, machine-gun posts, wrecked buildings and sometimes terrain features that might present special difficulties. Certain types of tape indicated the obstacles which the men could expect to encounter as they jumped over the parapet and began their advance.

The withdrawal, after an attack that had failed, was not as methodical as the advance. Henry Williamson describes British soldiers limping back from the fighting on the Somme:

Men, single and in couples, shuffling past them, answering no questions, men without rifles, haggard, bloodshot-eyed, slouching past in loose file, slouching on anywhere, anyhow, staggering under rifles and equipment, some with haws sagging, puttees coiled mudboiled around ankles, men slouching on beyond fatigue and hope, on and on . . . Stretcher-bearers plodding desperate-faced. Men slavering and rolling their bare-teethed heads, slobbering and blowing, blasting brightness behind their eyeballs, supported by listless cripples.

SNIPERS

Many soldiers feared death from a sniper's bullet more than they feared being hit by a shrapnel ball, a shell shard or a grenade. When they talked among themselves some admitted that being killed by a sniper was more worrying than going on a patrol, raid or attack. After all, in 'normal' combat there was a greater chance of being wounded than of being killed; statistics seemed to bear this out. However, the sniper's shot was almost invariably fatal since he was aiming at his victim's head. This was well known because British and Empire snipers sought for the same target.

The army had a definite sniping system from the time that trench warfare began late in 1914 and at that time steel loopholes were in use in the British lines in Flanders. Sniping activity was organized on the basis of special posts along the front of each battalion. Each post was responsible for a specified length of the enemy's front; from, say, 'The lone tree to the ruined windmill'. The post was manned throughout daylight by trained snipers, who were under the command of their own officer and NCOs. Their task was not only to snipe but to observe and each post submitted a daily report of the enemy's activities. A sniping post had a crew of four men, in two reliefs. In each pair, one man spotted through binoculars or periscope while his mate did the sniping. When a battalion was due to go into the frontline the snipers were sent up 24 hours ahead, for the sole purpose of making themselves familiar with the enemy's positions.

The sniping officer or senior sniping NCO chose the firing positions, though the experienced leader listened to his men's suggestions. Some snipers preferred to operate from shell craters in No Man's Land, others liked the natural camouflage of rubble. When working from a post in a trench, a British sniping team generally peered through the loopholes of the steel sniper's shield, as did the Germans. Even so, this tiny window had to be somehow masked so that daylight did not show behind it.

Generally the Germans used more common sense than the British and French in the way that they managed their parapet. The British parapet was certainly often irregularly shaped, as it needed to be when sniping posts were to be concealed in it, but more frequently it was fairly even. German parapets had a firm, regular line, but this was concealed with all kinds of rubbish and debris, smashed timber, mattresses, old iron and scattered bricks. It took a skilled eye on the British side to pick out a sniper's nest in this mess.

If German snipers were more deadly than their British or French counterparts it was because they operated in the same area for months, even years. Almost literally, they knew every blade of grass, every stone and sandbag on their front. If the enemy made any change overnight, these crack shots knew about it at a glance.

British and French snipers were only on the job when their battalions were in the frontline and even then the battalions were frequently moved from one sector to

A charge by the Guards on the Somme on 15 September 1916. Here the Coldstream Guards are leading, followed by the Grenadiers and Irish Guards. The artist accurately shows the difficult ground to be covered

R. Caton Woodville

another. The snipers had no opportunity to familiarize themselves with the enemy positions in the same way as the Germans.

How to Snipe 'Huns'

In January 1916 a specialist sniper officer contributed a section on his particular skill to a training pamphlet, *Notes From the Front*. Generations later, his advice tells us a great deal about sniping techniques. The anonymous officer begins by defining sniping. It is:

the art of: (i) finding your mark (ii) hitting your mark. With regard to (i) it is absolutely essential that the use of the telescope be taught from the stalking of Big Game point of view. If we had one Officer teaching it in every battalion of our army in France, we should kill a lot of Germans. Not only this, but the work of the Intelligence Officer would be greatly facilitated. With 4 good telescopes on every battalion front, very little can happen in the enemy line without our knowing it.

One specialist officer urged the use of a double loophole. A sniper's steel shield was placed in the parapet and 2 ft behind it a second plate was placed on grooves along which it could slide. This officer stated that not once in a hundred times could an enemy sniper get his bullet through both loopholes. He also advised the use of the drain-pipe loophole:

If put at an angle it is very difficult for a German to put a bullet down it. In fact, if it is put in low in the parapet, the brave Hun has to come clean over his parapet to shoot down it at all.

I am also keen on teaching our fellows to open loopholes sanely. I usually lie in front and it is rarely that I should not be able to shoot nine of every ten men who open them.

R. Caton Woodville.

Loopholes should be opened from the side and a cap badge exposed before they are

An impression of Australian troops during First Villers-Bretonneux, 4 April 1918. Advancing northwards from the town, the Diggers accounted for 4,000 Germans, killed, wounded or captured

R. Caton Woodville

looked through. If a German does not fire for 75 seconds one may conclude that it is fairly safe.

The use of snipers in attack is another point. If you have a man who can hit a model of a human head once in every two shots at 400 yards – and I will undertake to get most men up to this standard who can shoot decently – we shall kill some machine-gunners in our next advance. Also, when a German is shooting at our troops coming down a road, through an aperture made by the removal of a brick from a wall, as they have so often done, how useful to have a fellow who can put a bullet through that aperture.

When to shoot. Snipers should always select single men to shoot at and never a bunch of men. They should never shoot at a man who is looking towards them unless certain of killing him. They should never shoot at dusk or dark unless the man they are shooting at is alone and they are sure of killing him, otherwise their hidden position may be detected. They should always watch for shell bursts to fire a shot, the enemy's attention being distracted.

Finally, the officer insisted that men should be trained to understand and believe in their tele-sighted [sic] rifles. 'One brigade I had for instruction, on the third day of instruction, with 16 snipers shooting, got 18 hits on the model of a human head at 300 yards in the first 21 shots.'

There is no doubt that trained British snipers were good or that Australians from country areas were better. Natural and experienced marksmen from boyhood, these Diggers were accustomed to snap-shooting and many a momentarily careless German soldier fell to their prowess. How-ever, I believe that the German snipers were the most deadly of all, largely because of

their long familiarity with particular parts of the front. Many French veterans reluctantly conceded that they lost more men to German snipers than the other way round.

Soldiers on salvage duty clean up the battlefield. The man on the left is loaded with British gear, which would be used again, and on the right a heap of German equipment can be seen. A few bodies are removed for burial.
The quantity of salvage collected after a major battle was immense

Fortunino Matania

CHAPTER 6

*Machine-guns; Mortars; Blockhouses
and Pillboxes*

German machine-gunners and infantry emerge from a
blockhouse in Flanders to repel a British attack in the summer of
1917. Machine-guns were rarely fired from within a blockhouse

A. Forestier

German machine-gun posts caused great losses to British infantry and putting one out of action was a considerable feat of arms. Here Lance-Corporal Michael O'Leary of the Irish Guards attacks a post at La Bassée Canal, killing three Germans, capturing two and their gun. He was awarded the VC

Fortunino Matania

MACHINE-GUNS

German

The German army understood the potential of the machine-gun before all other armies and, as early as 1901, after years of experiment, an entirely new army branch was formed to handle them. At the outbreak of war the German army had 2,500 Maxim* guns in service and was receiving 200 new guns each month. This was just the beginning. By 1916 more than 3,000 a month were reaching the front and by September 1917 a massive 14,400 a month were being supplied.

Officially called the Maschinen Gewehr 08, the Maxim fired the standard 7.9 mm round and had a practical range of 2,200 yd and an extreme range of 4,000 yd. The weapon underwent several modifications, especially that of 1915 which gave it a bipod mount rather than the four-legged sledge mount.

Maxims were generally deployed in patterns of threes or fives, so that they could cover one another. Also, the system meant that should some be knocked out the others could maintain fire. Often sited in conjunction with pillboxes and blockhouses, the formidable Maxim was feared by Allied soldiers. It is not surprising that more high gallantry decorations were awarded for the attack and capture of machine-guns than for any other feat of battle.

During the winter of 1915–16 new machine-gun units were formed and trained with the intention of making the corps into a really powerful arm. They were known as *MG Scharfschützentrupps* (machine-gun marksmen sections) and were created from men who already had experience with machine-guns. They were then given a five-week training course at one of three machine-gun schools, with emphasis on machine-guns in the attack and on aggressive use of the guns in defence.

These units reached the front in February and March 1916 and were first used in March during the battle of Verdun. They were allotted to infantry regiments in offensive operations and to units holding difficult sections, such as in the Ypres Salient and on the Somme front. These gunners, among others, confronted the British and Empire troops when the British Somme offensive began on 1 July 1916.

---

* Its inventor was the American, Hiram Maxim, who evolved his machine mechanism in the 1880s. The British government gave Maxim his first order for machine-guns in 1887. It was for three guns for testing and, although they passed all tests stipulated by the government, the Maxim was not officially adopted. The same year Maxim tests made in Germany were attended by the Kaiser himself. He was so impressed that he ordered that it should be the gun for the German army.

The machine-gun marksmen companies consisted of one captain or lieutenant, two *Feldwebel* (sergeants), six gun commanders, (all *Unteroffiziere* or NCOs), twenty lance-corporals, forty gunners, one cyclist-orderly, one armourer, one medical corporal, one transport driver and six spare men. Imbued with an elitist spirit, these men fought with great bravery and to the death. It is no wonder, then, that the Allies suffered so severely at their hands.

British

The standard British medium machine-gun was the Vickers, a modified version of the Maxim. The gun was in such short supply and so under-valued that in 1914 only two were allocated to each infantry battalion. An associated problem was that soldiers detailed to operate the Vickers were given no special training so that when the few available guns were used during manoeuvres their potential was not demonstrated.

The main difference between the Maxim and the Vickers was that the latter, at 40 lb, weighed less and it had an improved mechanism. The gun was water-cooled with a barrel enclosed in a jacket containing 7 pints and with a condenser system to reduce water consumption. It used standard .303 ammunition, fed from a fabric belt holding 250 cartridges. The cyclic rate of fire was 450 rounds a minute and after 10,000 rounds or one hour's continuous firing, the barrel was worn out. Fitting a new one was a quick job for experienced gunners. Mounted on a heavy tripod, the Vickers was reliable and rarely jammed.

The Machine-Gun Corps was founded in October 1915 and from that time the Vickers guns were used increasingly and with great skill.

When the Vickers was located in a trench its pit was dug in the arc of a circle which corresponded to a wide field of fire. It was best to place the Vickers where they could lay down heavy enfilade or oblique fire. This created zones through which attacking troops would have to pass.

During the early war years, Vickers were generally kept back in or near the support line and from here they fired over the top of the front trench. A well established MG post had two or three small bunkers for the crew's shelter and for filling ammunition belts. During enemy shelling the gun was dismounted and taken below.

At times, a great deal was demanded of the Vickers guns and some crews were in non-stop action for hours on end. During the British attack on High Wood, Somme, on 24 August 1916, ten Vickers fired close to 1,000,000 rounds over a 12-hour period.

Medium machine-guns were too heavy and awkward to go forward with attackers, but by 1918 some units, especially Australian and Canadian ones, found ways for them to support an advance. Firing on map references provided by scouts and aerial observation, the gunners laid down almost continuous fire over the heads of their own infantry.

Machine-gun crews on both sides were a prime target for enemy artillery and for this reason British and Empire infantry disliked having Vickers near their lines. Because of enemy attention, the crews were often required to move their guns to alternative positions. This resulted in the infantry giving them the label 'the shoot, shit and scatter boys'. It was not uttered with bitterness; the infantry depended on the machine-gunners or 'Emma Gees', as they were known in army parlance.

An excellent impression of Lewis gunners in action. East of Ypres, German infantry broke through the British line but were stopped by the small party of machine-gunners in a 9.2-in shell crater. While one gunner fires, the other reaches for a fresh magazine

Artist unknown

The Vickers was so useful that it was fitted to tanks and armoured cars and even to aircraft. The Sopwith 1½-strutter was the first plane to receive a stripped-down version of the Vickers. Modified to fire about 1,000 rounds a minute, providing a stream of bullets, these aerial guns were synchronized to fire through the propeller arc.

Light Machine-guns

At the outbreak of war the Lewis* gun was adopted by the British and Belgian armies and the BSA company was turned over entirely to Lewis production. One reason for this was that six Lewis guns could be made in the time taken to produce one Vickers gun. Nevertheless, several high ranking British officers did not appreciate the Lewis' deadly significance and Lord Kitchener, as Secretary of State for War, set the number of LMGs required per battalion at only four.

On a bipod mounting, the Lewis had a circular drum magazine containing 47 rounds of .303 ammunition, the same calibre as that fired in the standard British rifle. The Lewis was tough and reliable and

---

* The Lewis was invented by Colonel Isaac Lewis, a retired officer of the US Coast Artillery. Despite several successful demonstrations to the US Ordnance Board, he could raise little official interest in the weapon. Lewis went to Belgium in 1913 and set up the Armes Automatique Lewis company to make his machine-gun.

Private John Lynn, Lancashire Regiment, serving his Vickers machine-gun during the gas attack of 1 May 1915 and beating off the German infantry attack. Despite the poisonous fumes, Lynn stayed at his post but died the following day. He was awarded the VC

E.A. Holloway

magazines could be quickly changed. When necessary, infantrymen handed over some of their own ammunition for the Lewis, which had a crew of two. The gun had a cyclic rate of fire of 400–600 rounds per minute but no crew, even with the help of a platoon as carriers, could carry enough ammunition to sustain such a rate. In practice, the Lewis was fired in short bursts.

David Lloyd George, when Minister for Munitions, quietly increased the allotment of Lewis guns to sixteen per battalion, but the infantry's demand for the weapon soon saw to it that every section of every platoon had one. This meant that there were about eighty to a full battalion. Even then, com-

manding officers, company commanders and platoon commanders tried by any means – foul when necessary – to acquire additional guns. The Lewis became the main weapon in any attack and every advance.

The German army formed light machine-gun sections in July, August and September ·1916 as an answer to the British Lewis gun. They were armed with the Bergmann automatic rifle, the barrel of which was the same as for the 08-pattern machine-gun. It was sighted to 400 m, as it was intended as a close-range weapon. The Bergmann was never as good as the Lewis and became overheated after firing 300 rounds rapid.

MORTARS

A mortar, strictly speaking, is any piece of ordnance designed to fire only at angles of elevation greater than 45 degrees. Invariably short-barrelled infantry weapons, they do not come under the classification of 'gun' or 'howitzer'. An ancient weapon which lobs its projectile from a high trajectory, the mortar came into its own during the Great War as a way of bombing trenches.

When the war started the Germans had only 150 mortars (*Minenwerfer*) but the British had none. The lack of these essential weapons proves yet again just how unprepared the British army was for a static war. The German weapons were made for three types of bombs, the 7.6 cm, 17 cm and the monster 25 cm. The 25 cm *Minenwerfer* fired a bomb weighing a massive 207 lb, the 17 cm a 109 lb bomb and the 7.6 cm a 10 lb bomb.

The *Minenwerfer* were skilfully made, with rifling, instrument sighting and recoil. The Germans first used them on the French front and having seen how effective they were at once put them into mass production. The High Command regarded the *Minenwerfer* as so important that it created seven *Minenwerfer* battalions to form a special reserve at the disposal of GHQ, which used them to reinforce particular sectors. These battalions were in addition to the divisional and battalion *Minenwerfer* companies.

In Britain, various 'experts' opposed the development of the trench mortar on the ground that it would be 'ineffective', but with Lloyd George's support production went ahead. The first model, which reached the front late in 1915, was little more than a piece of 4-in pipe, without rifling, sighting or recoil. A simple cylindrical bomb was dropped base first into the muzzle to fall onto a projecting pin at the base of the barrel. It detonated the firing charge which propelled the missile. The bomb, which carried to a maximum range of 1,500 yd, had a 25-sec time fuse but later an impact fuse was developed.

With the advent of the 3-in Stokes mortar in 1916 the British and Empire armies were much better armed. It could be roughly sited and ranged, but many bombs failed to explode. During my visits of exploration to Western Front, between 1956 and 1990, I have found at least 300 unexploded Stokes shells.

The early British mortar bombs were filled with metal scrap, nails and pieces of glass. These bombs appear not to have worried the Germans but the Stokes bombs, when they exploded, were effective. The 'toffee-apple' – a solid shaft surmounted by a spherical bomb – was another mortar projectile. It was supposed to land on its nose and explode on impact but many toffee-apples failed to explode and a large number merely broke into two pieces.

In contrast, the *Minenwerfer* bombs were well-made and fragmented on impact, at high velocity. They alarmed the British troops from the beginning and soldiers often talked about the danger from 'minnies' or 'rum jars'. The biggest enemy mortar bombs were known as 'flying pigs'. Essentially infantry weapons, *Minenwerfers* were fired from the frontline or support trenches and, reaching a high trajectory, their bombs fell straight into the opposing trenches. Experienced soldiers listened for the dull 'plop' sound made by the mortar when it fired and quickly sought shelter.

Major-General G.L. McNaughton, the Counter-Battery Staff Officer at Canadian HQ, invented a 200 lb trench mortar projectile of 9.45 in diameter which the Canadians christened the 'blind pig'. It had a maximum range of 400 yd and was unreliable, but it boosted the Canadians' morale. Sometimes they tunnelled out into No Man's Land to establish forward positions for the 'blind pig' mortar, in order to gain greater range.

BLOCKHOUSES AND PILLBOXES

The defensive positions known as blockhouses and pillboxes were miniature forts developed by the German army to give their trench lines added strength. The labels were applied by British troops. The rectangular blockhouse of reinforced concrete did indeed look like a block or giant brick, while the smaller construction, whether square, round or octagonal in shape, resembled the boxes in which chemists supplied their tablets. The first Australian reference to these positions, on 5 September 1917, describes them as 'pillar boxes'.

It is commonly supposed that the Germans operated machine-guns from within the blockhouses, but this is not the case. It was possible to fire from within some blockhouses through the narrow slits in the wall, but only with great difficulty. The slits were meant for observation and the blockhouses were essentially shelters for machine-gunners who remained safe, though shaken, during the fury of an enemy bombardment. When the gun-fire lifted, the gun teams quickly emerged to set up their Maxims on the top of the blockhouse or, more frequently, at the sides.

Blockhouses generally measured 30 ft along the front, with a width of 10 ft. They were sunk 3 ft into the ground and stood 7 ft above it. The front wall was up to 30 in thick. Massively strong, a blockhouse was virtually impervious to shell-fire; even a heavy shell would merely knock a large chip off an edge. The minor damage done to one of the blockhouses in Tyne Cot cemetery, Ypres Salient, provides a good example of the structure's ability to withstand direct hits.

The German army engineers who built the blockhouses placed them on high ground from where the machine-gunners could sweep the approaches which enemy infantry would be forced to use. Two good examples of this siting still exist in Flanders. Within Tyne Cot cemetery, or close to it, are the remains of five blockhouses, set in such a pattern that the gun crews at any one position could destroy enemy infantry trying to capture any of the others. The field of fire

Two forms of German blockhouses as drawn by an artist from descriptions by eyewitnesses of battle during Third Ypres, in the summer of 1917. The top drawing shows a blockhouse equipped with slits for machine-guns. Some British infantrymen filled the slits with shovelfuls of earth. A bomber threw grenades through the entrance, while bayonet men waited for the enemy to emerge. In the bottom drawing are two blockhouses, not equipped with slits. They were intended purely as shelters and the machine-gunners operated their weapons from the edges of the blockhouse and from a concrete wall built between the two shelters

A. Forestier

they enjoyed is obvious even now, though the blockhouses have sunk several feet into the soft Flanders clay. Two other blockhouses remain at Messines (Mesen), where they were built to cover the valley of the River Douve, an obvious route for enemy infantry attacking German lines.

The Germans operating from the blockhouses used entrances at the rear and sometimes at the sides as well. The only sure way of capturing a blockhouse was to throw grenades through one of these entrances. Firing a rifle or Lewis gun through the front observation slits might well cause casualties but could not guarantee capture. It was possible to push a grenade through some blockhouse slits, but more often than not the grenade would explode in the slit, causing little damage inside the blockhouse. Many blockhouses were blind except for the entrance at the rear.

In contrast to blockhouses, frontline pillboxes, which were much smaller than blockhouses, *were* machine-gun posts. However, the guns firing through the loopholes were generally Bergmann LMGs rather than Maxims.

In Flanders the water-logged nature of the ground made pillboxes preferable and the Germans built them in large numbers throughout their lines at Ypres and Messines. Many were covered with soil or camouflage but when bombardment laid them bare the Germans left them that way.

Murderous fighting went on around these blockhouses and pillboxes and the 'rules of civilized warfare' vanished. The Australians in particular, having seen so many of their comrades shot down by machine-gunners during desperate fighting, were in no mood to take prisoners. The Australian official historian C.E.W. Bean, is frank about it:

A good drawing showing a fighting patrol in action against a German machine-gun post protected by ruins and sandbags. The Germans had been firing over a crest at unseen targets when the raiders surprised them. In the right foreground is a dead German gun-horse with its driver and in the right rear is a wrecked German gun emplacement. The incident took place near Bapaume during the British advance of March 1917

S. Begg

When they have been racked with machine-gun fire, the routing out of enemy troops from behind several feet of concrete is almost inevitably the signal for a butchery at least of the first few who emerge, and sometimes even the helplessly wounded may not be spared.

A pillbox could be put out of action by a determined and skilful soldier. One of the most outstanding of such exploits was that of Captain Rupert Grieve of the Australian 47th Battalion during the battle of Messines on 7 June 1917. Machine-gun fire from a pillbox struck down all the officers of his company and half the men, as well as the crews of a Vickers machine-gun and a Stokes mortar which were advancing with Grieve. The attack was failing. Grieve took a bag of grenades and rushed forward from shell-hole to shell-hole, from time to time throwing a bomb at the loophole. With each explosion the enemy gunners ceased fire for a few vital seconds, giving Grieve time to get safely through the danger zone. He jumped into the enemy trench and, working his way towards the pillbox, threw another grenade close to the loophole. While the gunners were still cowering from this explosion Grieve rolled two grenades straight into the loophole. After they burst, Grieve slipped around to the pillbox entrance and found the crew lying dead or wounded around their gun. He then signalled his company to run up and occupy the trench. Soon after this he was badly wounded by a sniper but survived to receive the Victoria Cross.

A good example of a pillbox survives amid the shell-holes and craters of Hill 60, Ypres Salient.

The British army did not build

German officers and men in a blockhouse surrender to what are stated to be British troops, but were possibly Australian, in September 1917. The drawing has one serious technical flaw: the entrance would not be on the same side as the machine-gun because a shell could easily lob through it. If the entrance is supposed to be in the rear, where it always was, then the gun is facing in the wrong direction. However, other details are accurate. Note the officer's lead-loaded trench club

R. Caton Woodville

blockhouses of the German type. Their constructions were shelters rather than firing positions and were lined with 'elephants' – corrugated strips – in the same way as dugouts. The surviving examples look rather like Nissen huts in concrete. The concrete works were mostly built of one part cement, two of sand and four of stone. Iron strips added to the strength of the construction. Langhof Farm, between Bedford House cemetery and St Eloi, near Ypres, has a good example and there is another at Warneton (Waasten) on the River Lys.

Few British soldiers ever had the opportunity to fight from blockhouses or pillboxes because they were not features of the British frontline. The High Command feared that if the troops had such solid defences they would be less offensively-minded. The stated reason for not building them was that 'such works were not worth the labour or the cost'. In fact, the labour was available in massive quantity and the cost would have been slight. If cost really was the main factor in the decision not to build blockhouses and pillboxes then it must be assumed that the High Command valued the lives of the soldiers at less than that of the concrete.

CHAPTER 7

Tanks

Near St Julien, Ypres Salient, a British 'movable land-ship', as the
artist calls it, creates havoc among the terrified Germans in their
'stationary concrete fort'

A. Forestier

German soldiers throw grenades and fire rifles at tanks in vain attempts to stop the monsters which rolled towards them. This is a scene from the battle of Vimy Ridge, April 1917

A. Forestier

TANKS

The menace of the German Maxim machine-gun brought the tank into existence as a means of crushing machine-gun posts without losing hundreds of infantrymen. The British and French beat the Germans in the development of tanks, but even in Britain the idea met strong resistance from cavalry generals and others who lacked the imagination to see the potential of 'land battleships'.

After some tests with an armoured caterpillar tractor in February 1915, the War Office dropped the idea. Among the few far-sighted officers who kept pressing for mechanized armour was Lieutenant-Colonel E.D. Swinton, an engineer, who wrote a thesis entitled 'The Need for Machine-Gun Destroyers'.

Winston Churchill, another advocate of mechanized armour, formed a 'Landships Committee' which arranged further tractor trials. As a result, the first armoured vehicle appeared in July 1915. Nothing more than a tracked metal box, it was christened 'Little Willie'. It was, however, inadequate in several ways; for instance, it had little ground clearance and could not cross a gap greater than 8 ft. However, 'Mother' was developed on the model of 'Little Willie' and, after many problems had been overcome, it ran for the first time on 16 January 1916.

Shaped like a monster lozenge, 'Mother' was 33 ft long, 8 ft high and 8 ft 6 in wide. It weighed 28 tons and its 105 hp Daimler engine could push it no faster than 3.7 mph.

It had a crew of eight – the commander, driver, four gunners and two gearsmen, whose job it was to throw the tracks in and out of gear as the driver ordered. By this clumsy means the vehicle was steered. To communicate with friendly troops, the commander had to get out or shout through a megaphone from the door.

'Mother' became the Mark I 'tank', a word considered innocuous enough should the enemy hear of the new development. A description such as 'landship' would have been certain to arouse suspicion and alarm. 'Mother' passed all its tests but the generals were still lukewarm in their enthusiasm for the tank. Lord Kitchener dismissed the tank as 'a pretty mechanical toy' and pronounced that the war would never be won by such machines. The War Office ordered only forty tanks, but with Lloyd George's help – he was then Minister of Munitions – the order was raised to a hundred.

Half of the Mark Is were armed with a naval 6-pounder on each side and were known as 'male' tanks. The weapons were mounted in sponsons or half-turrets, which gave a wide field of fire. The 'female' tanks were armed with four side-mounted Vickers machine-guns and were intended for use against infantry. Both male and female tanks also had a single Hotchkiss machine-gun.

Before the tanks were ever in action, conditions for the crew inside them were frightful. The engine, in the centre, gave off fumes and heat and the noise was deafening.

As the tanks lurched, the sweating men were thrown heavily, bumped and bruised. Drums of oil and grease broke loose amid the jumble of equipment, rations, signalling equipment and pigeons, which were to carry messages to HQ.

By the end of August 1916 sixty tanks had been sent to France and were stationed at Abbeville, within reach of the Somme battlefield. The crews needed training and the tanks required testing, but General Haig saw them as morale raisers and wanted to use them at once.

One tank commander wrote:

> I and my crew did not have a tank of our own the whole time we were in England. Ours went wrong the day it arrived. We had no reconnaissance or map-reading, no practice or lectures on the compass, no signalling and no practice in considering orders. We had no knowledge of where to look for information that would be necessary for us as tank commanders, nor did we know what information we should be likely to require.

Forty-seven tanks were allocated for an attack on German-held Flers in September 1916. Imagine the appalling conditions for the crews of these 30-ton monsters. Without any sprung suspension, the tanks lumbered across rough country, with the crews coughing from the fumes, sweating from the 100-degree heat, in danger of being thrown into the uncovered working parts, and deafened by the clattering din. It was virtually impossible for the commander and men to communicate with one another except by hand signals. The commander had to leave the gunners to their own devices while he concentrated on driving the tank. He did this by giving hand signals to the man

Inside a French tank of 1917. Some men collapsed from the fumes. In the centre a gunner loads a 75 mm shell in to the gun's breach

J. Simont

The artist calls this 'a trial of strength between our movable land-ships and the stationary concrete forts'. In the summer of 1917, a British tank crushes an enemy machine-gun post near St Julien, Ypres Salient. It must have been a relatively small fort; even the heaviest of tanks could not have damaged a blockhouse

A. Forestier

One of the tanks engaged at Flers, in the first tank attack, September 1916. The early tanks needed rear wheels by which to steer

Frederic De Harnen

who changed the gears and to the two men, one to each track, who worked the levers at the rear of the tank to change direction. With an underpowered engine and unproven mechanism, fourteen tanks broke down before they reached the battlefield. The remaining thirty-six clanked to their battle assembly positions on the dark night of 13 September, astounding the assembling infantry, who had never before seen a tank. The following night they moved up to their battle start positions over ground so broken by shell-fire and old trench lines that there could hardly have been a man among the crews who did not anticipate disaster.

Of the thirty-six tanks, only half could be started at zero hour. Five more bogged down and about ten remained to play a part in the fighting. Their main operation was at Flers, where one tank drove down the street with cheering troops of the 41st Division. The first tank attack achieved little but it showed that tanks had a future.

One of the most graphic reports of the tank action at Flers appeared in *The Illustrated London News* on 9 December 1916:

From a communication trench had been dug a number of small trenches mostly composed of joined up shellholes, the whole providing a system of considerable strength, which would undoubtedly have cost our infantry appreciable loss, had not one of our Tanks quite unexpectedly appeared on the skyline and come lumbering towards the little strong point. The enemy holding the strong point had, of course, never seen or heard of such a thing as a Tank. Panic evidently seized them and a number, losing their heads completely, started running across the open.

Above the noise of bursting shells, the machine-guns of the Tank were heard to open, seemingly simultaneously. In less time than it takes to tell, the Boches had ceased to run; they all seemed to go over together like shot rabbits. The Tank never paused but went straight on over the trenches, firing right and left as it did so . . . Those who were watching it were alternately catching breath and gasping, as salvo after salvo of crumps seemed to burst clean on top of it. But nothing seemed to hurt it and it was still going strong when it vanished from our sight.

The same report said that the 'demoralised Boches' were petrified with fear, leapt out of their trenches at the approach of a tank and stayed immobile until British infantry took charge of them. Undoubtedly, tanks were terrifying and artists' impressions showing the monsters in action graphically capture the Germans' fear.

In the earlier part of 1917 newer model tanks did not perform well. At the two battles of Bullecourt, in April and May 1917, they were such a failure when they were supposed to be supporting Australian infantry that the Australians lost faith in them. In the Ypres Salient the tanks floundered helplessly in the mud. Nevertheless, the new formation became stronger and in June it was given the official name, Tank Corps.

Then came the battle of Cambrai on 20 November 1917. Here 474 Mark IV tanks were assembled, 376 of them fighting machines, the others for wire-clearing, carrying and communications. Since the enemy trenches here were exceptionally wide, each tank carried a 2-ton fascine of brushwood bound by chains to drop into the designated front, support or reserve tren-

During poor weather, tanks and Scottish troops loom out of a fog to crush German defences at Beaumont Hamel
at the end of 1916. A French correspondent said that Beaumont was a much more formidable stronghold than
Thiepval

R. Caton Woodville

ches and thus make bridges. Female tanks drove along the enemy parapets and machine-gunned the shocked Germans as they ran out from their dugouts. The other tanks smashed onwards and by midday the German commander was ordering a major withdrawal. Troops from General Byng's Third Army advanced up to 4 miles on a front of 6 miles.

The initial triumph was tremendous and the German infantry was terrified, but the British euphoria quickly evaporated. The Tank Corps commanders had wanted a reserve of machines to be held back to exploit the anticipated success but GHQ had denied their request. Now, 179 of the fighting tanks were out of action, the rest needed servicing and no reserves were available. To make matters worse, the cavalry, held for years to exploit just such an opening, were sent up hesitantly. On 26 November British infantry fought a major part of the battle, at Bourlon Wood, without tank support.

As the Germans massed to attack, Byng's position was desperate. On the southern part of the battle front the Germans retook part of their line. Total disaster for the British was averted by the Guards Division from Byng's reserve and by sixty-three tanks scratched together from a railway yard where they had been entraining. In a great tank achievement the new corps held the line but by 3 December both sides had suffered 50,000 casualties and were too exhausted to continue. Few of the Mark IV tanks at Cambrai saw any further action but the Mark V, which was much faster and

could be steered by one man, was used with great success by the Australians at the battle of Hamel, 4 July 1918. From that time the tanks were completely absorbed into the strategy and tactics of the Allied armies.

For the great British offensive, which began on 8 August 1918, 324 heavy tanks, 96 light Whippet tanks and 120 supply tanks were used. No decisive victory followed the initial breakthrough because of heavy tank losses and the failure to coordinate cavalry with tanks. For the first time, tank versus tank actions occurred during this period, with cannon-firing tanks defeating those dependent on their machine-guns.

The French were developing tanks at roughly the same time as the British –

German tanks of mid-1918. They had some advantages over British tanks, such as more machine-guns and a better command and observation turret. The artist has gone to some trouble to identify the tanks' features

D. McPherson

though neither of the Allies knew what the other was up to. French tanks first saw action in April 1917. The Germans had created a committee known as A7V to study designs for armoured vehicles, but neither its members nor anybody else in authority showed any great interest and nothing practical was achieved. It took the British use of tanks at Flers to galvanize A7V into action. The first tank was demonstrated to the General Staff on 14 May 1917 and was named after the committee, A7V.

The new vehicle was 23 ft long, 12 ft high and protected by $1\frac{1}{4}$ in armour. Powered by two Daimler engines, it carried a 5.7 cm gun at the front, and a 2.08 cm machine-gun on each side and at the rear.

The A7V was used for the first time at St Quentin on 21 March 1918 and when the war ended the Germans possessed forty-five tanks of this type. However, the Germans captured large numbers of British and French tanks including sixty British Mark IV tanks during the battle of Cambrai. All were fitted with the Germans' own 5.7 cm guns. The following year, during their March–April breakthrough, the Germans captured quantities of the Medium Mark A Whippet tanks. The German tank corps was four-fifths composed of captured British vehicles. The British female tanks were rearmed with 08 machine-guns, painted with German markings and called the *Beutepanzer*.

CHAPTER 8

Casualties; Stretcher-bearers;
Sickness and Self-inflicted Wounds

An exhausted French soldier has collapsed and his comrade,
though equally worn out, is about to carry him to safety. A scene
on the desolate battlefield of winter 1916

Georges Scott

A blinded Scottish officer is guided to an aid post by two of his men. The canvas bags they are carrying held grenades and ammunition

Georges Scott

CASUALTIES

No army involved in the Great War was prepared for the number of casualties or for the terrible illnesses that the conflict produced. The army medical services, from the unit medical officer at his regimental aid post to the field hospital and base hospital, were overwhelmed by the casualties of 1914. The British army suffered 86,000 dead or wounded by the end of the year and French and German casualties were many times greater because of the larger size of their armies. Successive battles were blood baths and just a few statistics show the extent of the slaughter.

The 1st Battalion Queen's Royal Regiment sent 850 men into the battle of Gheluvelt, Ypres, on 31 October 1914. A lieutenant brought out the 31 survivors. At the end of First Ypres, 18 November 1914, the average strength of the original battalions of the BEF was 1 officer and 30 men, instead of 40 officers and 1,000 men.

At Neuve Chapelle, Flanders, the British army lost 13,000 men between 10–13 March 1915 and in Second Ypres, April–May 1915, British casualties amounted to 50,000 men. On the first day of the battle of Loos, northern France, 25 September 1915, several battalions were wiped out and total casualties at the end of the battle, 8 October, were 60,000. Casualty figures for the first day of the battle of the Somme, 1 July

A scene of concentrated suffering as wounded French soldiers queue for attention outside a Poste de Secours, while on the right some German prisoners await their turn

Artist unknown

Lance-Corporal Joseph Tombs, King's Liverpool Regiment, won a VC at Rue du Bois on 16 June 1915. He crawled out under fire to bring in four helpless, wounded men. On the fourth occasion he looped a rifle sling around his neck and the casualty's chest and dragged him back to the trenches

W. Avis

1916, totalled 54,470: 19,240 killed; 35,493 wounded; 2,152 missing (i.e. now known to be dead); 585 taken prisoner. One in every two men of the attacking force of 143 battalions was a casualty. When the battle ended on 18 November the British and Empire armies had suffered 420,000 casualties. During the battle of Arras, April–May 1917, 30,000 British soldiers were killed and 128,000 wounded.

Third Ypres began on 31 July 1917. When it ended on 6 November the British and Empire armies had suffered at least 400,000 casualties. During the fighting on the Western Front for the entire 1914–1918 period, the British and Empire armies lost 118,941 officers and 2,690,054 men as battle casualties. More than half of all British and Empire soldiers on the Western Front suffered some kind of wound in battle.

Service on the Western Front carried risks other than being killed or wounded by enemy action, as a simple statistic shows: 3,528,486 men were listed as sickness casualties.

Statistics, especially in large numbers, tend to obscure the suffering to individual soldiers, but this can be understood by a visit to Lijssenthoek cemetery, near Poperinge in the Ypres Salient, where virtually every soldier of the 11,000 buried there died of wounds. That is, they survived long enough to be brought back to casualty clearing stations, field ambulance and field hospitals, where they died. The collective suffering which this cemetery represents is immense, yet nearly all visitors to the Ypres Salient go to the famous Tyne Cot cemetery, where lie men who were killed in action, while very few go to Lijssenthoek.

STRETCHER-BEARERS

Few war artists or illustrators produced paintings or drawings about stretcher-bearers or wounded men being tended on the battlefield or in hospital, perhaps because 'authority' discouraged them from doing so. Yet, paradoxically, many of them drew soldiers lying dead on the field of battle. Perhaps they were then seen as heroes and a fit subject for publication in a work of art, whereas wounded men indicated suffering, which was best not emphasized. Some illustrations are shown in this section, but where they do not exist word-pictures will have to suffice.

A soldier wounded on a Western Front battlefield might have been considered still to be fit enough to leave it as a 'walking wounded'. Otherwise he had to lie where he fell until picked up by stretcher-bearers. The pre-war theory about stretcher-bearers in action differed from the actual practice. In 1914, an infantry company then had an establishment of four bearers and it was assumed two could carry a wounded man. In reality, on the Western Front at least four were necessary and, if a casualty had to be carried for any distance through mud, eight men, and even ten were needed, so that each pair could have a spell from the utterly exhausting labour. Extra men were sent up from reserve to act as bearers and help the RAMC field ambulances but only rarely were enough available. In any case, stretcher-bearers themselves became casualties, even when carrying white flags or wearing Red Cross brassards.

Bringing in a wounded man on a stretcher was not merely a matter of getting him off the killing field. He then had to be carried along the trenches to an aid post. This meant negotiating the traverses and fire-bays, crowded with men intent on their task. Working and carrying parties needed to thread their way through the busy trenches and the stretcher-bearers had no priority of way. Often the only way they could move with their burden was to hold the stretcher high above their heads. They were glad when their charge was unconscious but often the wounded man would be writhing in pain and perhaps screaming.

The bearers delivered the casualty to the Regimental Aid Post (RAP), which was usually in the second or third line of trenches. Here the Regimental Medical Officer (RMO) and his assistants applied or changed a dressing or gave injections. The doctor rarely attempted surgery beyond amputation and passed the wounded man back, again by stretcher-bearer, to the Advanced Dressing Station (ADS). Here another team assessed the wound and the doctor might decide on amputation or give treatment for haemorrhage or gas poisoning.

The ADS was so placed that it might be possible for an ambulance to pick up casualties for the next phase of the evacuation. This was to the Casualty Clearing Station (CCS) serving the particular division, where many operations were performed and professional nursing help was available. The surgeons staffing a CCS might perform 2,000 operations a day during a big attack.

A surgeon and dressing station orderlies attend to casualties on 4 April 1918. The episode took place during the first battle of Villers-Bretonneux and in this, as well as the later battle, Australian units were the most prominent

A. Forestier

The Flemish town of Ypres was probably the most famous landmark on the British sector of the Western Front. German guns destroyed its famous buildings and by night the ruins took on a ghostly appearance, never forgotten by the soldiers who were there

Christopher Clark

Overleaf
*Main picture:*The assault on Vermelles. In the first months of the war much hand-to-hand fighting took place in towns and villages because trenches and wire did not exist and the armies could easily get at each other.
Places changed hands frequently. The Germans captured Vermelles, northern France, in October 1914.
On 1 December the French recaptured the château and part of the town in ferocious fighting, which is shown here.
British troops were in action near Vermelles on several occasions

Georges Scott

Inset: A German trench captured by the French in October 1915

François Flameng

Above: Six-in guns on 'Percy Scott' mountings. The artist was attracted to these guns by their gaudy camouflage and wrote at the time, 'War, as far as the artillery is concerned, is developing into a vast fancy dress ball, with immunity from destruction as the prize for the best costume'
Fortunino Matania

Right: The church in Albert with its famous 'leaning Virgin', in August 1915. British medical orderlies are about to scrub a field stretcher
François Flameng

When it was possible – and when patients were strong enough – they were moved further back to field hospitals, general hospitals, stationary hospitals and, finally, to base hospitals.

Stretcher-bearers finished their task at the CCS and headed back for the line to collect another casualty. The hardest part of the stretcher-bearers' job came after a major battle when so many wounded men littered the field that it was not possible to rescue all of them. Then the bearers had to decide which casualties seemed to have the best chance of surviving. A man still living but with his intestines spilling out from a gashed stomach wound was not a good bet. Despite the judgments the bearers made, they sometimes reached the RAP with a dead man on the stretcher. Equally, they might bring in an apparently hopeless case who survived. They became hardened to their work – else they would have gone mad. Many of them became casualties from the sheer physical strain of doing their exhausting job day after day. One bearer, Private Bill Corey of the Australian 55th Battalion, was four times awarded the Military Medal for his bravery. He was the only soldier of the war to be so decorated.

Inevitably, in the confusion and under great pressure – and often in the dark – the bearers missed many wounded men. Some of these managed to drag themselves into a shell-hole where they were certainly less likely to be wounded again but where stretcher-bearers might not see them. Here they bled to death or slipped deeper into the often flooded hole and drowned. Even so, there were remarkable cases of men staying alive for a week or more until found.

Some men died slowly and often in agony in positions from which no attempt to rescue them was possible without the loss of even more men. Sometimes the Germans recognized a Red Cross flag waved from a trench and allowed bearers a brief time to bring in wounded, but more frequently the firing continued. Then, from some shell-hole in No Man's Land, wounded men cried out in pain and begged to be helped. Some pleaded to be shot to end their suffering. Unable to bear a mate's torment, many a soldier dashed out on a mission of mercy only to be killed himself by an enemy sniper.

The Royal Army Medical Corps analysed the causes of wounds received by British soldiers in this way: shells, 59 per cent; bullets, 39 per cent; grenades, 2.19 per cent and bayonet, 0.32 per cent; the other 0.49 per cent were not specified. However, these statistics apply only to men received into the RAMC's care; no analysis of those killed on the battlefield was possible. I consider that bayonet wounds resulted in a greater number of deaths than might be indicated by these figures. A wound from a bayonet was almost instantly fatal, so that the victim did not have long enough to be included in wounded statistics.

SICKNESS AND SELF-INFLICTED WOUNDS

During 'quiet' periods – that is, when there was no major attack by either side – a British battalion lost an average of thirty men a month through death, wounds or sickness. The sickness might be trench feet, frost-bite, bronchitis, influenza, pneumonia, bladder or bowel infection, food poisoning, eye infections or dysentery. Diarrhoea, which sapped the men's will and health, was a constant menace but in its 'milder' forms was not considered serious enough to evacuate a sufferer. At times, especially in winter, few men in the front trenches were really fit. On a night when there was little firing the main sound that could be heard over the battlefield was that of men coughing.

Many men 'disappeared'. Soldiers used the expression 'blown to kingdom come' to describe the day a comrade vanished during a bombardment. A soldier actually hit by a shell exploding on him literally vanished; there was not a trace of him to be seen. The same fate befell many a soldier crouching in a hole when a shell dropped into it. One survivor of a bombardment lost a mate and went in search of his remains; all he found was his denture.

The effect of explosions differed wildly. Some left limbs, head, torso and organs strewn around. Yet, other shells, bursting among a group of men, would kill all of them with shards and splinters but leave their bodies more or less intact. At other times the concussion, especially in a confined space, was enough to kill men without actually wounding them.

The recurrent strain and tension resulting from spells of duty in the front trenches and in attacks on enemy lines, together with the constant danger of being killed or maimed, was too much for some men. Some lost their reason and became gibbering idiots. Others suffered from 'shell-shock', which at that time was an ill-defined disorder. Yet others were sent back from the line with their medical condition described as NYD(N); this meant 'not yet diagnosed (nervous)'.

A percentage of men killed themselves rather than face yet again the torment of the trenches. The usual method of suicide was to place the muzzle of the rifle against the head and press the trigger with a bare big toe. A much larger number of men found escape through a self-inflicted wound, SIW in army parlance. Common SIWs involved a bullet through the foot, the calf or the fleshy part of the thigh, or blowing off a thumb or forefinger. Generally, there was an attempt to pretend that the wound had been caused by an enemy bullet during action. No doubt many such deceptions were successful. Occasionally a SIW was passed off as an accident in training.

Wounding oneself was a capital offence – that is, it was punishable by death by firing squad, following court-martial. After treatment in hospital, soldiers known to have committed a SIW, or suspected of having done so, were kept in a special SIW compound at Boulogne, a place of great shame. Most of them proceeded to court-martial. I know of none who was executed

A French battalion commander, a major, is hit during an advance during the battle of Champagne, October 1915. A captain, about to assume command, pauses briefly to say, 'Bon chance, mon Commandant!' In a shoulder-to-shoulder attack such as this casualties were inevitably heavy

J. Simont

A wounded soldier has died before bearers can take him into a field hospital. A chaplain reads a prayer over his body. One of the bearers (right) who helped to carry him from the battle field is a German prisoner. A scene in Flanders

Fortunino Matania

but many were sentenced to long terms in army prisons. If the truth were known, countless thousands of soldiers were tempted to find an escape through a SIW but fought down the temptation.

Large numbers of men evaded duty, if only briefly, by feigning or inducing illness. Swallowing certain brands of toothpaste in quantity would increase the temperature to above normal; vomiting could be induced to the point of producing blood by a strong saline solution; eyes could be inflamed by rubbing cordite into them. One RMO claimed to have discovered more than eighty ways in which soldiers had tried to persuade him to mark them 'excused duty'. Anybody who understands the conditions of life on the Western Front will not be too quick to condemn the desperate men who disabled or killed themselves to get away from what seemed to them like hell itself.

CHAPTER 9

Gas Attacks; Mining and Craters;
Signallers; Runners

Crouching in a tunnel, French officers listen for sounds of enemy
mining activity. They will then blow a camouflet and entomb the
Germans. One officer wears the Medaille Militaire

Christopher Clark

The French were among the first to use dogs in war. Some sought out wounded men on the battlefield, others were canine sentries. This drawing shows a message-carrying dog racing through a gas attack in 1917

Charles W. Wyllie

GAS ATTACKS

In April 1915 the Ypres Salient had a north–south base of 10 miles and pushed into German-held Flanders for about 5 miles. It was held by Canadians and British troops on the centre and right and by French Territorials and their Algerian troops on the left.

The German guns bombarded Ypres and other targets in the morning of 22 April but the entire front was quiet in the afternoon. At 5 p.m. the enemy guns opened again and this time sentries on the left of the salient (the north side) drew attention to low yellow–green clouds drifting slowly towards the Allied lines. Many puzzled men looked at the thick woolly stuff and some officers, anticipating that German infantry were advancing behind a smoke screen, shouted 'Stand-to!'

It was chlorine gas, not smoke. The Allies really should have been expecting it, for the Germans had already used gas against the Russians. German soldiers who had recently been taken prisoner disclosed that a gas attack was imminent and British patrols had reported seeing gas cylinders in position. The Allied troops had been given no warning and now they paid the penalty. As the vapour reached them, it burned their throats, caused pains in the chest and choked them. 'What followed is practically indescribable', reported Sir John French:

> The effect of the gas was so overwhelming that the whole of the positions occupied by the French divisions were rendered incapable of resistance. It was impossible at first to realise what had actually happened. Fumes and smoke obscured everything. Hundreds of men were thrown into a stupor and after an hour the whole position had to be abandoned, together with 50 guns.

The suffering and panic-stricken French Colonial troops and the French Territorials fled, leaving a dangerous 4-mile gap in the Allied line. Canadians and British troops, on the right of the gap and mostly unaffected by the gas, were outflanked by the German infantry advancing behind their gas. They fought hard but the Germans captured a large part of the Salient before the Allied line was cobbled together. There might well have been a decisive enemy breakthrough but the German troops were to some extent held back by their own gas. Also, their High Command had not expected such a dramatic success and was not ready to exploit the gap.*

* While it is popularly believed that the Germans were the first to use chemical weapons, this dubious honour belongs to the French. They fired tear-gas grenades in the first month of the war. The Germans were nevertheless a long way ahead of the French in the development of chemicals and gas and in October 1914 they fired shrapnel shells in which the steel balls had been treated with a chemical irritant.

With no gas masks available, attempts were quickly made to find a protection against this alarming new weapon. It was found that the ammonia in a urine-soaked pad held to the mouth and nose neutralized the chlorine. Soldiers were told that handkerchiefs dampened with a solution of bicarbonate of soda gave a rough and ready protection. In less than three days 100,000 pads of cotton waste wrapped in muslin were available and tie-on masks of lint and tape were made.

French troops used what was known as the 'hypo-bath and straw method' of defending themselves against gas. Handfuls of hay were kept in or on a barrel in the trench, together with bottles of hypo (sodium thiosulphate). When the gas alarm was given the men saturated a bunch of hay and held it over the nose and mouth until the gas had passed. This crude protection was apparently successful but obviously the French soldiers could not fight with one hand over their face. By mid-July 1915 the troops were well supplied with efficient gas masks and 'anti-asphyxiation respirators'.

In June, some British troops were issued with the 'smoke helmet', a bag shrouding the entire head with goggle apertures for vision. Another protection was a large gauze pad tied with tapes, with an extra flap to cover the eyes. Each man was given a bottle of hyposulphite solution in which to soak the pad.

There rapidly followed a grey flannel hood impregnated with Phenol and fitted with formica eyepieces. Next came the 'tube-helmet', a flannel hood with the addition of a rubber-tipped metal tube which the soldier gripped between his teeth to assist in exhaling.

All the gas-protection devices were primitive until the introduction of the box respirator as standard issue late in 1917. Kept in a box-bag on the chest, the respirator could be quickly fitted over the face and held in place with straps. A tube channelled the gas into a filter tin in which charcoal and chemical filters neutralized the poison.

From the gas users' point of view, chlorine had a defect – coughing and choking limited the victim's intake. Phosgene was found – by the Allies as well as the Germans – to be more effective. Much less of it was needed to incapacitate a soldier and it had a delayed-action effect. Men who seemed quite well collapsed and died up to 48 hours after exposure. A mixture of chlorine and gas – known as 'white star' gas – was specially effective because the chlorine provided the vapour to carry the phosgene. White star was much used on the Somme front.

The British army raised Special Gas Companies, totalling 1,400 men, under Lieutenant-Colonel Charles Foulkes. They were ready for action by September 1915 and British poison gas reached the front that month in large, heavy metal cylinders, each of which was slung from a pole and carried by two men. However, their contents were not called gas. That word was not mentioned and the gas warfare men were warned that using it could result in punishment. The code name for the gas was 'accessory'.

The Special Gas Company manned 400 gas emplacements at Loos on the evening of 24 September. By turning the cocks on the cylinders they were to discharge chlorine gas – and smoke – intermittently for 40 minutes before the British infantry assault. The emission began at 5.50 a.m. next morning, but wind conditions deteriorated and so

Soldiers in weird 1915 masks bring up water, rations and ammunition during a gas attack and under shellfire. The officer is Temporary Captain E.M. Allfrey, who was later awarded the MC for his courage and outstanding service

J.H. Valda

much gas was blown back into the British trenches that more British soldiers than Germans were affected by the gas. Pandemonium broke out in some trenches and the attack failed, though not merely because of mistakes with the gas.

The Germans, always one step ahead of the Allies with poison gas development, were determined to achieve a strategic breakthrough with it. In mid-1917 they used mustard gas in shells for the first time. It caused serious blistering to the skin and respiratory tract several hours after exposure and protection against it was difficult. It remained potent for several weeks, thus making stricken areas untenable for troops.

Wearing a gas respirator in action made a soldier significantly less effective. Much more effort was required and men became exhausted by heavy exertion, such as digging, running and heaving. A soldier's visibility was also impaired and many men suffered from stress while wearing masks.

Mustard gas caused the greatest number of gas casualties in the British and Empire armies, followed by chlorine, phosgene and chloropicrin. Before the mustard gas period, the gas casualties from April 1915 are estimated at 13,000 but poor records were kept and the true figure is probably much higher. Between July 1917 and November 1918, the mustard gas period, 124,702 British and Empire soldiers were evacuated to hospital with blisters, burns or temporary blindness; 2,308 of these men died. The American army and marines suffeed 71,552 gas casualties. German gas casualties are thought to have been 200,000.

In 1986 five warrant officers of the Belgian army's Bomb Disposal Squad were killed when a Great War mustard gas shell exploded while they were attempting to defuse it after it had been dug out of a farm field.

Two British soldiers were awarded the VC for their courage during gas attacks. On 1 May 1915, the Bedfordshire and Hertfordshire Regiment was gassed while holding trenches at Hill 60 and in some places the men were driven out. As a result, one trench was held single-handed by Private Edward Warner. Reinforcements were sent to him but they could not get through the gas. Warner came out for men and led them to the trench, which he continued to hold, though he was ill and exhausted.

The following day, Private John Lynn, DCM, Lancashire Regiment, was holding a position in the Ypres Salient with his Vickers machine-gun. The Germans were advancing behind chlorine gas mist, which badly affected Lynn but he remained in action with his gun. When he could not see clearly enough from his original position he moved his gun onto the parapet, from where he stopped the enemy advance. Both soldiers died from their exposure to the gas.

MINING AND CRATERS

Mining was the laborious and dangerous task of tunnelling under enemy lines to plant a massive mine to blow up trenches and men and gain a tactical advantage. German engineers and miners began burrowing as the British and French armies settled into trenches late in 1914.

On 20 December they blew ten mines under trenches manned by Indian soldiers at Festubert. Half a mile of front erupted in a staggering explosion that caused much loss of life and damaged the morale of the entire British army. Already traumatized by the horrors of modern war, the men were now terrified of being blown up and some stricken units were withdrawn.

On many parts of the front soldiers resorted to crude attempts to discern enemy tunnelling. One method was to drive a stick into the ground and hold the other end between the teeth and feel any underground vibrations. Another method involved sinking a water-filled oil drum into the floor of a trench. Taking turns, soldiers lay in the muck and lowered an ear into the icy water, which conducted sound more readily than earth. Also, underground vibrations caused the water to quiver.

The British army started mining later than the Germans, although Britain was renowned for its mining engineers and its professional miners were probably the best in Europe. Despite the mass of skilled labour available in Britain, the first troops to be used as miners were men of the Royal Engineers, who were given only three days' training.

German mining has been detected under a British trench in the Ypres Salient and it is quickly evacuated. The drawing provides a good example of a type of trench revetting, together with a platformed fire-step. Bayonets are fixed because an enemy infantry attack usually followed the blowing of a mine

R. Caton Woodville

These French sappers of 1917 are listening for tell-tale sounds of enemy mining activity. They have sunk into the ground specially sensitive instruments which relayed the 'tap-tap-tap' of tools. The French could then blow a camouflet to wreck the enemy tunnel

Christopher Clark

On the authority of Lord Kitchener, John Norton Griffiths MP, known as 'Empire Jack', recruited some special mining companies from among tunnellers and miners in Britain. Independently-minded and often middle-aged, these men were ready enough to do the job but they did not regard themselves as soldiers and some pointed out to officers that military drill was not part of their 'contract'.

When a mine was being sunk the infantry in reserve was brought up to provide carrying parties for the spoil sent up by the miners.

Miners worked in pairs in 8-hr shifts and generally by candlelight. One man gouged earth out of the face and passed it to his mate who stuffed it into sandbags. From the tunnel mouth other men dragged out the bags on ropes. Conditions were appalling, even for professional miners accustomed to the discomfort of the work; the miners did their work in narrow, poorly ventilated tunnels. Sometimes there was so little oxygen that the candles would not burn and many miners collapsed or struggled on despite severe headaches. On many occasions miners came across the decomposing bodies of men killed in earlier fighting and then had the extra task of extracting the remains and reburying them in quicklime.

Miners debated the relative characteristics of chalk, clay and runny brown mud. Chalk was the cleanest and most stable but it more readily transmitted sound. Another problem was getting rid of the white spoil, clear evidence from the air that tunnelling was in progress. Clay, especially blue clay, came away cleanly in lumps and was easily cleared away. Runny mud was abominable because it oozed, caused tunnel supports to collapse and was difficult to shovel.

As mining intensified, the risk of opposing miners digging into each other's tunnels became ever more likely. Every hour or so miners pressed their ears to the walls to listen for tell-tale scraping or thumping sounds. They were well aware that the enemy was doing the same. When counter-mining was detected, a race developed to finish the work and detonate before the enemy. Sometimes it was enough to blow a camouflet – a local explosion carefully calculated to destroy the enemy mine and bury the miners. Occasionally, miners from one side broke into an enemy tunnel and savage fights with picks and shovels occurred. A few British officers gained a reputation by

A lance-corporal and an officer of the 5th South Lancashire Regiment were preparing a mine for blowing when they heard voices from a German counter-mine. The team hurried to complete the mine, which they blew while the Germans were still working on their mine

Margaret Dovaston

penetrating German mine systems and driving off the enemy miners before destroying their work.

Blowing a mine could produce great advantages, apart from killing enemy soldiers and wrecking their defence line. An explosion threw out a great mass of soil, rock and debris and as it fell it produced artificial heights around a deep crater. The moment that the spoil had fallen to earth – but long before the dust had settled – troops were rushed to the crater line to establish observation points and machine-gun posts. Both sides used crater lips to strengthen their defences and sometimes to provide a jumping-off point for a local attack.

Every crater was given a name, and often it was reminiscent of a great natural explosion. On the Cambrin sector, for instance, Etna and Vesuvius were located. Near Beuvry, Midnight Crater could be found and on the Givenchy front the Royal Welsh gave the name the Red Dragon to what was probably the largest German mine on the Western Front.

Blown in June 1916, its actual cup – the hole made at ground level without taking the spoil into account – was 40 yd across. Its full dimensions are not accurately known. About two-thirds of a company of Welshmen died in the blast.

The name RWF was given to triple overlapping craters blown by the Germans near the La Bassée Road and captured by the Royal Welsh Fusiliers. Some of the crater names are still well known, the Caterpillar at Hill 60, for instance.

Mining became more ambitious. The largest single mine of many at Hill 60 contained 2,700 lb of explosive. On 15 July 1915 a charge of 5,000 lb was blown at Hooge. Two of the biggest mines blown at the beginning of the British Somme offensive on 1 July 1916 each contained 24 tons of explosive.

Mining preparations for the Messines offensive of 7 June 1917 went on for about a year. British, Australian and Canadian miners laid twenty-one mines at the end of tunnels ranging in length from 200 ft to 2,000 ft and at depths of 50 ft to 100 ft. Two mines failed to explode but in the others more than one million pounds of explosive went up. The mine at Maedelstede Farm contained 94,000 lb of explosive and that at Spanbroekmolen 91,111 lb. Known as the 'Pool of Peace', the water-filled crater at Spanbroekmolen still exists as an awesome memorial of the war's destructiveness. It measures 430 ft from rim to rim and the pool is 40 ft deep.

SIGNALLERS

Military historians, war correspondents and official histories have all justly given the infantry the greatest attention in their writings. The greatest number of high decorations for gallantry went to infantrymen, an indication that it was they who faced the greatest danger. The work of the gunners, the medical personnel and, to a lesser extent, that of the miners and tunnellers and pioneers, has been acknowledged. However, the desperate, difficult and often dangerous work of the army signallers has been given inadequate attention.

The signaller in the field was a soldier of much importance. Right from the beginning of the war, signallers were using Morse keys, field telephones, Lucas lamps, flags and heliographs to pass information forward to the fighting units and back to various HQs. They soon found that the pre-war methods, flags, lamps and heliographs, all viable in the open warfare of the first few months, were useless in trench warfare. A signaller would not survive for a second were he to stand up to use his flags; lamps could only safely be used at ground level and hence had a short range; heliographs worked from a tripod stand, which made them all too conspicuous and in addition they needed sunlight. For long periods, there was a dearth of sunshine on the Western Front.

In the early days of trench warfare, signallers laid cables along the floor of trenches but when this practice resulted in many wires being broken by soldiers' boots, they attached the lines to the trench walls with staples. This, too, was not successful as soldiers hung such heavy weights on the wire or staples that breaks occurred. In any

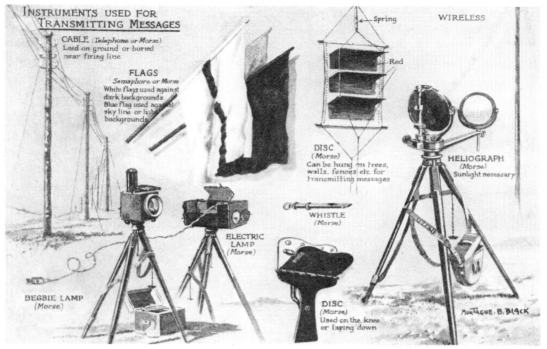

In April 1918, an artist drew the various types of signalling equipment used in the British army. All the mechanical methods depended on Morse code

Montague Black

case, wall wire was vulnerable to shell-fire. The signallers' next step was to bury cables to a minimum depth of 18 in, later changed to 3 ft. This laborious task led to much disruption in the trenches. Also, the cables, even when sheathed in lead or steel, could still be broken by a mortar shell lobbed into a trench.

Trenches developed so many festoons of signalling wire that they impeded movement and then officers protested. This sometimes resulted in lateral signal wires being banned in trenches. The signallers then had to stretch their wires behind and parallel to the trenches. But the wires needed to cross communications trenches and were often wrenched and broken by high loads being carried along these trenches. The signallers solved that problem by mounting an

inverted V-shaped piece of timber across the communication trench and fastening their wires to that.

All messages received at, or emanating from, a trench signals station were officially secret. Signallers were under orders to reveal the contents of messages to no one other than the officer designated and they had to be passed to him immediately. Messages had to be precise, and guesswork, even under danger and pressure, could be punished by court-martial. Errors could be costly and sometimes fatal.

Battalion and company officers highly valued a fast, accurate and reliable signaller. When there was some doubt about an important message getting through by telephone or telegraph a runner carried the same message.

At Hooge, on 11 August 1915, a communications dugout was blown in and the two operators were wounded.
Private S. Wilson of the 1st East Kents took over and under day-long shell-fire maintained communications. He was
awarded the DCM

Francis E. Hiley

Signallers were trained in encoding and decoding messages. The need to maintain communications, under all circumstances and at all cost, was drilled into them at every signals school they attended. Breaks in telephone lines caused by enemy gun-fire had to be repaired, even during bombardments. Many brave signallers perished trying to carry out this duty.

Signallers worked closely with gun batteries and artillery observation posts, which were always well forward or high up, and therefore in dangerous places. Maintaining the telephone link between observation posts, usually known as OPs or O.Pips, and battery was one of the most responsible tasks any signaller could have.

The British army neglected wireless throughout the war and laid cables everywhere. Signallers, with their wagons, followed every advancing infantry unit, laying down their cables for mile after mile, all the way from rear HQs to forward posts. Many of these brave men, working in exposed positions, were killed on duty.

The Army Pigeon Service was quite widely used, but mostly for routine communications. The pigeons were reliable and hardy and often flew through heavy bombardments. However, they had a serious limitation. Pigeons fly only from somewhere 'away', back to a known base, hence they could be used only from the frontline to the rear, not the other way round.

In one vital way the British telephone communication system at the front was deficient, though this was not the fault of the field signallers. Battalion HQs were not linked directly to one another, even when several of them were operating as neighbours in the frontline. Battalion HQs could contact one another only through brigade HQ, which was further back. Under the French system, battalion HQs were connected by telephone, so that colonels could more rapidly respond to crises as they occurred. It was possible for one battalion to support another within minutes or to be warned of an imminent enemy attack which it might not know about. The British frontline telephone system made this impossible and valuable time was wasted.

RUNNERS

In a sense, runners were messengers, in that they were carrying messages from one place to another. There is a common belief among people interested in the First World War that any soldier could be an efficient runner. Certainly, every private soldier at some time was detailed for duty as an orderly room runner in camp, but men used as runners for trench or battle duty were among the most rigorously trained specialists in the army.

Runners were required to reconnoitre their battalion front 24 to 48 hr before the unit moved up. This scouting was generally done by teams of eight runners working in pairs. They were identified by red arm bands around their left forearms. The runner needed a clear, visual picture of the terrain and area covered by the latest, intricately marked trench map. He had to know how to read that map, on which battalion and company HQs were precisely pinpointed, so that no time would be lost when guiding officers and men into their locations. Runners were also trained to use a compass and encouraged to exercise their initiative. Runners often became casualties and in this emergency any soldier might find himself doing a runner's duty in hurrying with a message from battalion HQ to the frontline or vice versa.

Gas-masked French troops leaving their trenches for an attack near Verdun, 1917

Georges Scott

A British gunner officer with field telephone sets off to follow an infantry advance and report its progress to his own guns. Signallers follow him with reels of telephone cable. The bag on the officer's belt contains his gas mask. The scene is from the end of 1916

Frederic De Harnen

A British observation post in captured German trenches, during the British Somme offensive of August 1916

François Flameng

CHAPTER 10

Grenades

British soldiers using 'jam-pot' grenades in August 1915. At this date grenades were primitive and caused more noise and smoke than actual damage

Frederic Villiers

Atop a barricade in a part-captured German trench, Private T. Brown of the Gordon Highlanders throws grenades which disable many enemy and force the others to retire. Note his webbing grenade pouches. Brown was awarded the DCM

H. Ripperger

GRENADES

The hand grenade stood out as the principal weapon of hand-to-hand fighting on the Western Front, especially from mid-1915. So many military reports and journalistic accounts of the fighting used – and still use – the jargon phrase 'attacking with the bayonet' that this became the popular conception of combat. In fact, in most close-quarter fighting the main task of the rifle-and-bayonet man was to protect the bombers 'at all costs'. Many more bomb duels than bayonet fights took place.

However, the British army was not ready for grenade warfare in 1914. The War Office planners did not see much need for the weapon and only a few men of the Royal Engineers were trained in the use of the one model available. This was hand grenade Mark 1, a percussion type. A canister with a 16-in cane handle, it was armed by the removal of a safety pin through the top. When it was thrown, the handle and linen streamers ensured that it landed nose first, so that the striker was forced into the detonator.

A serious handicap was that the grenade could explode prematurely if it was knocked against something in the act of throwing. With the long handle in a trench it was all too easy to have a fatal accident.

Dissatisfied with the Mark 1 or, more usually desperate for any sort of grenade, soldiers made 'jam-tin bombs'. Literally a jam tin, the bomb was packed with dynamite or gun-cotton, bits of scrap metal and glass. It was set off by a detonator and a length of Bickford's fuse projecting through the top of the tin. By rough calculation, each inch of fuse gave about $1\frac{1}{4}$ seconds delay.

Slabs of gun-cotton or dynamite fastened to wooden bats made a type of improvised percussion grenade which became known as the hairbrush or racket bomb from its shape. Later, an official version of the hairbrush was made and became the grenade No. 12.

Another early model was the Newton Pippin. Its fuse was ignited by tapping it sharply against the handle of the entrenching tool. A similar bomb was fired by striking it against the side of a match-box.

Hand grenade No. 15, a ball type, was made in large numbers in the latter part of 1915 – 500,000 a week by the end of September. However, the wet conditions in the trenches destroyed its early reputation and it was rarely used after 1915. In all, fifty different types of grenade were designed throughout the war, but by far the most famous and most effective was hand grenade No. 5 or Mills bomb, introduced in May 1915.

The Mills became available in quantity but the demand was so great that it was not in universal use until 1917. Weighing $1\frac{1}{4}$ lb, the Mills bomb had a serrated surface so that when it exploded it broke into segments for greater lethality. The thrower removed the safety pin while still holding down the striker lever. This sprang off when the grenade was thrown and the bomb exploded 4 seconds later. Soldiers were taught to use a bowling action when throwing from a trench or shell-hole.

A British bomber prepares to throw an early type of grenade, with streamers attached to steady the missile and lengthen its flight.

Artist unknown

By the end of 1915 grenades were leaving the factories at the rate of 250,000 a week. In newspaper advertisements, the public was asked to contribute to war funds by sending one guinea to pay for six Mills bombs.

Tactics and handling of Mills bombs were constantly changing. For instance, *Notes from the Front*, issued in January 1916 made these observations:

The best bomb to use in a bombing attack is the 'MILLS'. It is the only bomb that can be retained in the bomber's hand until he has an opportunity to throw with advantage. All bombers must be supplied with a left-handed glove or finger stall. We discovered that the men's fingers got absolutely raw from pinching in the split pin and drawing out the ring from the Mills bomb. It would be a great

improvement if the Mills bomb could be supplied with a larger ring and better device than the present split pin. [This was done.] The casualties among the bombers are necessarily very great. It is absolutely essential that every Officer, NCO and man in the ranks should be instructed in how to throw a Mills Bomb.

Tests for grenade-throwers under instruction were demanding. The soldier had to throw ten dummy grenades from a standing position into a 4 ft wide trench 30 yd away. Of these five bombs had to land in the trench. From a kneeling position he had to lob five out of ten bombs from a distance of

Second Lieutenant A.J.T. Fleming-Sandes saves his line during the battle of Loos, 29 September 1915. The Germans were only 20 yd away when Fleming-Sandes attacked them with grenades. Fully exposed, he was twice badly wounded but rallied his shaken men. He was awarded the VC

J.H. Valda

20 yd. Standing in a trench he was required to land five grenades in another trench. Finally, he had to throw grenades over traverses into a fire trench and land five out of six on target.

Another version of the Mills followed in 1917, the No. 36M grenade, which, after being filled with explosive, was sealed by dipping into shellac to prevent deterioration. It was also given a stronger base plug, for use when being fired from a rifle discharger. The No. 36M had a 7-second fuse when used in this way and a range of up to 225 yd.

Mills bombs were carried to the front trenches in boxes of twelve, with a separate small box inside containing the detonators, which were fitted into the grenades close to the line. The soldier carried them, in the

Private W.B. Harris, a Canadian soldier, dropped a grenade while in the act of throwing it. To save a nearby mate and to prevent the grenade from blowing up a stock of bombs, Harris threw himself onto the exploding grenade. He was severely wounded and was awarded the DCM. Similar acts resulted in the VC being awarded

A. Pearse

Second Lieutenant A.B. Turner, Berkshire Regiment, leads a bombing attack along a communication trench during a critical action near Vermelles on 28 September 1915. He was awarded the VC, but died of wounds received in the action

S.T. Dadd

beginning, in a bandolier-type leather belt. However, by 1916 green canvas buckets were on issue to carry grenades in an attack. Each bucket contained twenty-four Mills bombs which could be easily taken from the bucket, prepared and thrown. The British uniform pockets were too tight to carry grenades but the capacious Australian pocket could hold six grenades.

Prodigious quantities of grenades were thrown. The greatest bomb fight of the war took place on 26–27 July 1916, at Munster Alley on Pozieres Heights, and lasted for $12\frac{1}{2}$ hr non-stop. The Germans used every sort of bomb – cricket-ball grenade, stick grenade, egg bombs, as well as rifle grenades. Australian soldiers, together with some Welsh and British troops in the early stages, threw 15,000 Mills bombs. The regimental bombers of the Australian 5th Brigade became casualties almost to a man. Other bombers collapsed from exhaustion.

More than 70 million Mills grenades of all marks were used on the Western Front in the period 1915–18. To this total can be added another 35 million hand grenades of other types.

As with everything else, the Germans began the war with better grenades than the Allies. The German army had sent observers to the Russian–Japanese War in 1904 and they reported that hand grenades would be essential in any European war. As a result, in 1914 the German army had 70,000 hand grenades and 106,000 rifle grenades.

There were several types, principally the *Stielhandgranate* (stick bomb or potato masher), the *Diskushandgranate* (disc grenade), the *Eierhandgranate* (egg grenade), and the *Kugelhandgranate* (ball grenade). Among the several variations of the ball

Germans who had hidden in pillboxes and dugouts were firing at the backs of advancing British troops. Three-man mopping up teams were detailed to deal with this menace. Here, in May 1917, the bomber throws Mills bombs into a dugout, while the riflemen wait to deal with any survivors. Note the supplies of German grenades in the captured trench

S. Begg

Several hand-to-hand bomb, bayonet and fist encounters took place during the fighting for Combles, Somme, in October 1916. Here three French soldiers attack a post containing six enemy. They won their private battle

Lucien Jonas

Skilled trench raiders in action. Two bayonet men lead the way along an enemy trench, while a bomber lobs a grenade across the traverse. The bayonet men then took advantage of the enemy confusion and ran in. In the right rear a periscope is being used to check progress, while another man has a rifle grenade ready for use.

D. McPherson

grenade was a segmented type, known to the British as the pineapple grenade.

All the German grenades, except the disc type, were activated by a time fuse; the disc was a percussion bomb and as any sharp knock on any one of the four protruding caps could set it off the Germans themselves did not like it. The egg grenade weighed only 11 oz and could be thrown 50 yd, rather further than the British grenades.

The stick bomb was so effective and so popular among infantrymen that it became virtually the standard issue grenade. Apart from a few made to explode on impact, stick grenades had either 5.5- or 7-second fuses; the delay was stencilled on the handle. Storm troops used fuses of only 2 or 3 seconds, making it impossible for their enemy to take cover before the explosion.

The stick grenade consisted of a cylindrical case filled with black powder and fitted to a hollow wooden handle, through which ran the activating cord. The soldier unscrewed a cap on the end of the stick and pulled the cord sharply, thus setting the fuse burning. In practice, he did all this while throwing. Because of the handle, the grenade could be thrown up to 60 yd. Carriage

was an initial problem so the grenade heads were fitted with a hook and the bombs could then be carried on the belt. Many soldiers carried their grenades in sandbags slung saddle fashion around their neck.

The German army produced gas grenades (*Handgasbombes*) of several types, all containing a liquid that was spread by a small bursting charge. In addition a smoke grenade (*Nebelbombe*) was issued. The heavy white smoke it gave out was supposed to hinder the enemy rather than to cover the movements of the user, the usual purpose of smoke.

Rifle grenades were no more accurate for the Germans than for the Allies and in 1916 they abandoned them. However, experiments continued and in 1917 a discharger cup was issued for attachment to the rifle muzzle. A grenade was placed in it and fired by an ordinary cartridge to a range of 200 yd.

To achieve greater distance, a grenade discharger mounted on a platform (*Granatenwerfer*) was used. The two-man crew could carry the two-piece 88-lb weapon in an attack. They had carriers with boxes of the fin-tailed grenade, which could be propelled more than 300 yd.

CHAPTER 11

Air War Above the Trenches

Flight Sub-Lieutenant R.A.J. Warneford VC, with his Morane-Saulnier, an aeroplane prominent in early 1915. The drawing shows the uniform of the time and an RFC flier in characteristic pose. Warneford, famous for having shot down a Zeppelin, was killed when his plane crashed on 17 June 1915

Christopher Clark

Aerial combat in 1914. A German observer, above, exchanges revolver shots with a French observer. These first primitive war-planes had no armament and flew at less than 60 mph. This is a German version of 'a fight in the air'

H. Moloff

AIR WAR ABOVE THE TRENCHES

The air war fought above the Western Front has often been glorified as a form of knightly combat, in which the victor saluted the vanquished as his flimsy machine spiralled earthwards. Fliers were said to have had such great respect for their foes that they collected the flying helmet, gloves and boots of a dead enemy and dropped them at low level on his home airfield, in recognition of his courageous end. This was a myth. Such foolhardy behaviour was punishable and the number of such occasions could be counted on the thumb of one hand.

Dogfights between opposing fighter pilots were deadly and no mercy was shown. Fliers were encouraged to follow a victim down to make sure that he did indeed crash or land in enemy territory where soldiers could capture him. The shooting down of unarmed reconnaissance planes was routine, as it had to be. After all, the pilots of scout planes were in effect spies. They spotted enemy guns and ranged their own artillery onto them. They took photographs of the German trenches and, through the rapidly evolving science of aerial photography and analysis, staff officers were able to build up a systematic picture of the enemy defensive system. German scouts were engaged in exactly the same work. No wonder, then, that both sides considered unarmed scouts fair game.

Many thousands of air fights took place, vastly more than in the Second World War. During this war few soldiers ever saw a dogfight but on the Western Front there could have been few who did not witness this enthralling spectacle. The aircraft were slow, flying at little more than 60 mph, and many combats took place at only a few thousand feet. Also, most fights were actually over the trenches or only a short distance to the rear, not hundreds of miles away from the ground fighting front, as in the Second World War. In the Second World War also, airfields were generally a long way behind the front. During the Great War they were within a few miles of the rear trenches.

To say that the Allied British–French–Belgian armies and the Germans started the war with an air *force* is going too far. They had nothing more than a small collection of flying machines made of wood and canvas and the daring fliers took them up only on reconnaissance. The aeroplanes were slow and clumsy and a few fell apart in the air. Some were pushers – that is, the engine and propellor were behind the wings and behind the pilot. It was not unknown for the engine to drop off.

The first Royal Flying Corps (RFC) aircraft to land on French soil was the BE2a of Lieutenant H.D. Harvey-Kelly. He touched down at 8.20 a.m. on 11 August. The headquarters of the RFC went to France on 13 August, just four days after the British Expeditionary Force. An Henri Farman, piloted by Second Lieutenant Louis Strange, which crossed on 16 August, was the only RFC aircraft to be fitted with a machine-gun, a Lewis carried on a mounting in the front cockpit. The gun and its installation was Strange's own idea and on

A British airman in hot pursuit of an enemy plane over the trenches in March 1916. The pilot was Flight-Commander R.J. Bone. Note that the cheering soldiers had not at this time been issued with steel helmets

John de G. Bryan

22 August, with Lieutenant L. da C. Penn-Gaskell as gunner, he took off from Maubeuge to chase an enemy aircraft. The German escaped and Strange's commanding officer decided that the Lewis gun's weight had prevented the Farman doing battle with the German. He ordered Strange to get rid of the gun, an action which the aggressive lieutenant considered absurd.

On 25 August three machines of No. 2 Squadron forced an enemy plane to land for the first time, and the German flier destroyed his machine. Later that day another enemy plane was forced down and captured intact.

Nobody knows which was the very first combat involving a single-seater scout, but one of the first took place on 28 August when Lieutenant Norman Spratt in a Sopwith Tabloid forced down a German two-seater, a feat he achieved purely by manoeuvre, since his Sopwith was unarmed. Spratt cleverly flew above the German and made feint attacks, which convinced the German that he was beaten.

The enterprising Louis Strange worked on his Henri Farman and on 2 October made this interesting entry in his diary:

Fixed a safety strap to leading edge of top plane [wing] so as to enable passenger to stand up and fire all round over top of plane and behind. Took Lieut. Rabagliati as my passenger on trial trip; great success. Increases range of fire greatly and I hear that these belts are to be fitted to all machines.

Later that month Strange and Rabagliati were aloft again, this time in an Avro 504, also fitted with a safety strap. On 16 October the pair chased and fired at an Aviatik two-seater but it escaped. Despite the orders of his CO, Strange mounted a Lewis gun on his Avro and he and Rabagliati went looking for prey.

The primary role of aircraft was reconnaissance. In all previous wars and even during the autumn and early winter of 1914–15, the cavalry supplied information about enemy movements. Soon, the belts of fixed defences prevented any forward movement of mounted men. Even if they had been capable of reconnaissance, the cavalrymen could never have spotted all the enemy's guns and railway movements, and this duty also fell to the new breed of airmen.

Aircraft development was rapid as all the fighting powers sought to gain superiority. In the beginning, scout planes went up

The artist entitled this drawing 'The Cruise of the Dead'. The RAF plane was directing artillery when it was attacked by six Albatros scouts. The British pilots brought down one enemy and a second plane from the same squadron helped to drive the Germans back across their own lines. However, the first RAF plane, A3816, did not return to its own lines and nothing was heard of it until the following night. It was found in a field 50 miles from the scene of combat, with pilot and observer dead in their seats. Doctors said that both men had been killed instantaneously. It was surmised that the machine had flown itself in wide circles, drifting with the wind until the petrol ran out, when it glided to a landing

Joseph Simpson

without guns and pilot and observer were armed with nothing more than a revolver and a rifle respectively. Some crews carried grenades and *flêchettes* (darts) which they tried to drop onto enemy fliers beneath them. Surprisingly enough, they scored some hits, but not very many.

The RFC's Order of Battle for 10 March 1915 listed eight squadrons, consisting of eighty-five aircraft of twelve different types. Of these, the only real fighter was No. 16

Squadron's single Vickers FB5. The FB stood for fighting biplane. Actually designed to carry a machine-gun, the FB5 was a two-seater pusher with a ceiling of 9,000 ft. FB5s probably made up the first homogeneous fighter squadron, No. 11 Squadron RFC, which reached France on 25 July 1915.

On that very day, the first VC for air combat was won by Captain Lanoe Hawker of No. 6 Squadron. Late in the afternoon,

While patrolling in a Vickers aircraft near Achiet, on 7 November 1915, 2nd Lieutenant G.S.M. Insall pursued an enemy plane. The German pilot lured Insall over a battery of ack-ack guns but Insall flew too close to his enemy for them to open fire. In the ensuing duel, Insall's gunner twice fired into the German aircraft and it crashed. Insall was awarded the VC

W.A. Avis

Hawker took off from Abeele, near Poperinge, in a single-seater Bristol Scout with a single-shot cavalry carbine mounted on the starboard side of the fuselage. Over the Ypres Salient, Hawker attacked an enemy two-seater and forced it to dive away. Continuing his patrol, Hawker flew over Houthulst Forest, near Ypres, where he attacked another two-seater and damaged its engine, forcing it down. Finally, over Hooge he took on an Albatros two-seater and shot it down in flames. All three of Hawker's opponents were armed with machine-guns so his triumphs, the most outstanding up to that time, were all the more remarkable.

The fitting of Lewis guns to a swivel on top of the upper wing of a biplane gave the pilot a real chance of shooting down an enemy plane. However, fighter pilots longed for the ability to be able to fire along their line of flight. This would entail shooting through the whirling propellor arc, and that seemed mere fantasy. A crude synchronization system had been evolved by a French designer but it often broke down, leading to smashed propellors. A French flier, Roland Garros, and his mechanic fixed metal plates to the propellor of his Parasol in order to deflect those bullets from his own machine-gun which did not pass through the synchronization system. The propellor's inner faces were channel-shaped and 8-mm solid copper bullets did not fragment on impact.

The pilot and observer of a British scout plane had failed three times to drop bombs onto a German despatch
car. In August 1915. The pilot flew daringly low, while his observer machine-gunned the car, killing the driver and
forcing the vehicle to crash and overturn

Gordon Crosby

An interesting close-up of a 'bomber' in action. Lieutenant G.I. Carmichael had only one bomb, weighing 100 lb, which his gunner dropped over the side of his plane onto the railway line at Menin station. Carmichael gained a reputation for his artillery observation work and won the DSO

W. Avis

On 18 April 1915, when Garros was on patrol over enemy territory, a bullet from the ground struck the Parasol's engine and Garros glided to a landing. Frantically, he tried to set fire to the aircraft and destroy its secrets but the Parasol would only smoulder and smoke. German soldiers took Garros prisoner and his aircraft was shipped off for inspection by German technical officers. It was shown to Antony Fokker, a Dutchman in German service, who improved on the Garros system. He developed a mechanism which interrupted the gun's firing every time the propellor was opposite the muzzle. The Fokker interrupter gear revolutionized air fighting.

Air tactics became a major factor and the Germans initially had the advantage. Flying Fokker monoplanes, in 1915 the German aces Max Immelmann and Oswald Boelcke collaborated to exploit speed, height and concealment to develop tactics.

The next step was to build aircraft specifically as fighters to protect the scouts, which had to fly level and steadily in order to do their job. Over Verdun, early in 1916, the German fighters gave their scouts virtual immunity from attack. The French found an indirect riposte by building bombers to attack German infantry and artillery. The German fliers, leaving their scouts to shoot down the bombers, returned to find their scout planes destroyed. Finally, the French won the air battle over Verdun with the Nieuport Scout, an armed and faster reconnaissance plane. The scale of air fighting over Verdun was more intensive than elsewhere on the Western Front because it took place in a small arena, with hundreds of aircraft engaged at any one time.

Meanwhile, on the British front, on 14 January 1916, RFC HQ ordered that a scout plane must be accompanied by at least three fighters and that all must fly in close formation. So great was the threat from the German Fokkers that on 7 February 1916, twelve fighters were detailed to protect one BE2C on a reconnaissance flight.

When the battle of the Somme began on 1 July 1916 the RFC had a total strength of twenty-seven squadrons (421 aircraft), with four kite-balloon squadrons and fourteen balloons. The squadrons were organized into four brigades, each of which worked with one of the British armies.

An important innovation was the introduction of tracer ammunition. While some experimental work had been done before the war, the first successful tracer ammu-

Over Poelcapelle on 20 June 1915, Flight-Lieutenant W.H. Ackland was attacked by a German biplane, but Ackland outmanoeuvred his opponent, so that his observer could machine-gun him and send him down. Enemy anti-aircraft fire ('Archie') set fire to the British plane and both RFC officers were badly burnt, but Ackland landed his plane safely. He was awarded the MC

John de G. Bryan

nition was the SPK Mark VII.T, known as the 'Sparklet'. The RFC began to use it in July 1916 and instantly found it useful. With every seventh round a tracer was fired so the gunner–pilot could see his stream of fire and adjust his aim accordingly.

The RFC held its mastery of the air until autumn 1916, when the Germans conceived the idea of operating their best pilots in squadrons. Simultaneously, they were issued with the new Albatros fighter, which was sturdier, faster and more manoeuvrable than the British aircraft. As a decided bonus, the Albatros fired two guns through the propellor. With the new, deadly squadrons the Germans began for the first time to strafe the Allied infantry in their trenches. This led the infantry to mount Lewis guns on any kind of available wheel, which was itself mounted on a stand, so that they could return the fire of the fast-moving pilots. In a frenzy of aircraft development, the Germans introduced the fast and man-oeuvrable D-type fighters. Deployed in large numbers, they took back control of the skies.

A notable British victim of German technical supremacy was Major Lanoe Hawk-mer. In November 1916, at the age of twenty-five, he was shot down and killed by Baron Von Richthofen, his DH2 being out-classed by the German's Albatros D11. The German fliers were so deadly that British losses mounted alarmingly, climaxing in 'Bloody April' of 1917.

Formation flying became essential for suc-cess and survival in aerial combat. It was based on the 'flight' – six aircraft flying to a pattern. Usually, the flight commander was in front, with an aircraft on either side forming a V. To the rear and above were two other planes and alone behind them was the sub-leader. Despite the formation, there was an overriding principle that in combat the pilots operated in pairs, one to attack, the other to defend. Formations became larger, especially on the German side. They created the *Jagdgeschwader* (fighter squadrons), soon to be called circuses, which moved to various parts of the line as emergencies dictated.

The surviving RFC airmen breathed a collective sigh of relief when their own new aircraft, the Sopwith Camel, the SE5 and other machines proved to be the equal of the German aircraft. Even the highly regarded Fokker DVII could not redress the balance for the Germans, and with their airmen draining away, they never again controlled the skies. This meant that in 1918, Allied aircraft were more frequently able to attack enemy troops with impunity. In April 1918, the RFC became the Royal Air Force and indeed it had become a *force* in its own right.

At the Armistice, Sopwith Camels and SE5As equipped most of the RAF single-seater fighter squadrons, together with a few Dolphin units, while the Snipe was begin-ning to arrive in numbers. The two-seater squadrons had the splendid Bristol fighter.

Britain and Germany developed bombers for making strategic strikes against cities and industrial installations but, although they caused civilian casualties, they were little more than nuisance raids and they had no effect on the outcome of any campaign on the Western Front.

The Air Fighting Rules of Oswald Boelcke
The best position in aerial combat is that where one can shoot at the enemy from close range without his being able to reply. Therefore:

Climb before the attack and dive from the rear. Altitude imparts speed in a dive and widens the patrol area.

Use natural cover – clouds and the glare of the sun.

Attack when the enemy is unsuspecting and preoccupied with other tasks.

Hold fire until the enemy is within range and squarely in your sights.

The basic offensive manoeuvre is to turn more tightly than your opponent, thus coming into position on his tail.

Never turn your back and run from the enemy, turn and face him with your guns.

To parry an attack from ahead, turn directly towards the opponent and present as small and as fast a target as possible.

To parry an attack from behind, enter and maintain as tight a turn as possible to make it difficult for the enemy to stay on your tail.

Foolish acts of bravery are fatal. Fight as a single unit and obey the formation leader's commands.

The Aces

In all the new flying corps, the air war brought to prominence certain men who excelled in combat. These fliers were the 'aces'. No service officially recognized the term but it was the generally accepted word to describe an airman who shot down a certain number of enemy aircraft.

To distinguish between outstandingly successful warplane pilots and those who were merely average, the French started to use 'ace' to describe those who had shot down five or more enemy. Roland Garros was the first ace. Other air forces adopted the same standard but the Germans did not consider a flier an ace until he had despatched ten enemy planes.

The Royal Flying Corps (and then the Royal Air Force) did not officially adopt the

An artist's vivid impression of a German flier falling from his plane after a mid-air duel. Airmen had no parachutes and being pitched out of an open cockpit during a dogfight was far from rare

Parys

ace system because senior officers considered that all its fliers were outstanding. However, unofficially, the great Hun-killers such as Mick Mannock, Albert Ball, Billy Bishop and others were known as aces. Large numbers of German fliers were shot down and the stringent regulations of the day ensured that claims of kills had to be verified. This was generally not difficult, since dogfights took place within sight of thousands of witnesses.

A victory score was not necessarily a true measure of the quality of an ace. Max Immelmann ranks only ninety-first on the German list but he was one of the most illustrious of German war pilots.

Some idea of the high casualty rate among pilots can be gained from a table of victories achieved by the leading ace of each nation. The top scorer for Britain and the Empire was Major Edward Mannock with 73;* for Germany, Rittmeister Manfred von Richthofen, 80; for France, Capitaine Rene Fonck, 75; for the United States, Captain Edward Rickenbacker, 26; for Italy, Maggiore Francesco Baracca, 34; for Belgium, 2nd Lieutenant Willy Coppens, 37; and for Austro-Hungary, Hauptmann Godwin Brumowski, 40. The number of victories achieved by the ten leading aces in each nation: British 562; German 497; French 385; Austro-Hungarian 224; Italian 193; American 143; Russian 115; Belgian 84.

No fewer than 785 pilots of the RFC/RAF had a score of five victories or more. Many pilots may have shot down more enemy aircraft than are included in their official scores, since much of the air fighting took place over German-held territory where kills could often not be confirmed. Several veterans gave the credit for some of their victories to new pilots.

Major Mannock was the leading British ace not only in terms of score but in most other ways. Born in 1887, Mannock was an inspector with a British telephone company in Turkey and when that country sided with Germany he was interned. On 1 April 1915 the Turks repatriated Mannock, partly because he was in ill-health and had poor eyesight. Strangely, the Turks considered that at the age of twenty-eight he was too old to be an effective soldier. Back in Britain, Mannock was accepted into the Royal Engineers but the RFC fired his imagination and the exploits of the young Captain Albert Ball inspired him.

He transferred to the RFC in August 1916 and was soon known as an almost fanatical hater of Germans. As a patrol leader he had no equal in any of the combatant air services – even the Germans conceded this. Mannock carefully planned his operations, with the result that his formation was never taken by surprise. When his friend James Byford McCudden, VC was killed on 9 July 1918 – in an accident – Mannock swore vengeance against the Germans and renewed his onslaught against their pilots.

In his last combat Mannock made an attack on a two-seater and then left the *coup de grâce* to a novice, 2nd Lieutenant D.C. Inglis. As Inglis shot down the enemy aircraft a German soldier on the ground fired a lucky round which hit Mannock's petrol tank and he went down in flames. His grave was never found. He had shot down 73 enemy pilots and had been awarded the VC, the DSO (three times) and the MC (twice).

With forty-four victories, Captain Albert Ball is eleventh on the list of British aces but

---

*Mannock's award of the Victoria Cross on 18 July 1919, after his death, credited him with 59 victories. Ira T. Jones, who served under Mannock in 74 Squadron, was an early biographer and claimed 73 victories for him. In 1990, following exhaustive research, Shores, Franks and Guest, in *Above the Trenches*, produced a total of 61, including observation balloons. Of this total, 47 were outright kills, not shared victories. With just one of the three squadrons with which he served, No. 40, Mannock flew 200 operational sorties. If Mannock had fewer than 72 victories, the figure claimed for the Canadian Billy Bishop, he does not rank as the leading British and Empire ace. Mannock admirers are unlikely to give way on his traditional 73 victories, no matter how much research is carried out.

Captain A.M. Miller, seeing British cavalry held up by German machine-guns, drew their fire and engaged the gunners. The cavalry was able to advance without further loss

J.P. Campbell

he might well be the best known, because he was one of the few RFC fliers to get any national publicity. A second lieutenant of the Sherwood Foresters, Ball joined the RFC in January 1916 and, flying a BE2C, he was engaged on reconnaissance and artillery spotting. In May, in another squadron, he was given a Nieuport Scout, a splendid little fighter which Ball loved. His first confirmed success came on 2 July 1916 when he shot down a Roland C11 on the Mercatel–Arras road. His virtually private war on the German air force began on 16 August when he attacked five enemy planes, driving down three of them. On 21 August he attacked seven Roland C11s, shot down one and evaded the fire of the other Germans. That same day he attacked another five Rolands and shot down two of them.

Following the formation of fighter squadrons, Ball took his Nieuport to No. 60 Squadron, whose CO gave him a roving commission. His dangerous technique was to get very close to the belly of his oppo-nent, pull his Lewis gun back to the near vertical and fire a long burst. This tactic rarely failed.

Appointed a flight commander in No. 56 Squadron, Ball flew an SE5 and had a Nieuport for his 'personal use', should he feel like a lone scrap. He was flying the Nieuport on 6 May 1917 when he brought down an Albatros. Late on the evening of 7 May he was seen diving into cloud during combat with a German single-seater. His plane crashed but it is not known for certain which German flier brought it down. Ball died in the crash but was found to be unwounded from the combat.

Still only twenty years of age at the time of his death, Ball had been awarded the VC, the DSO (three times), the MC, the Croix de Guerre, Legion d'Honneur, and the Russian Medal of St George.

Ball fought with great courage and skill and became the model for the fighter pilots of his day.

INDEX

(page numbers of illustrations are shown in italics)